A READING OF
GEORGE HERBERT

Enamelled cross, xii c., B.Mus.: Grapes, Serpent, Tau, Widow of Sarepta

A READING OF
GEORGE
HERBERT

*

Rosemond Tuve

UNIVERSITY OF CHICAGO PRESS

CHICAGO, ILLINOIS

THE UNIVERSITY OF CHICAGO PRESS, CHICAGO 37, ILLINOIS
W. J. Gage & Co., Limited, Toronto 2B, Canada
Faber & Faber, Limited, London, W.C. 1, England

To
Carleton F. Brown
and
Edwin A. Greenlaw

PREFATORY NOTE

BECAUSE of the simultaneous publication of this book in both England and America, a note is perhaps necessary regarding certain critical issues which are in it assumed to be familiar matters of controversy, but which may be (as such) very much more familiar to American than to British readers. Some of the most vigorous and most influential modern literary criticism in America—often that concerned with 17th-century writers—shows the attitudes, presuppositions, or controversial positions herein noted as 'modern' positions and variously supported or attacked. These sets of ideas cannot be equated with 'The New Criticism', although most of the 'New Critics' take some or all of the positions discussed. The quickest way to refer a reader to controversies so lively and new points of view so acutely and voluminously defended that they have gone far to transform the practice of criticism as well as the teaching of literature, is to cite the critiques and bibliography in R. W. Stallman, *Critiques and Essays in Criticism, 1920-48*, New York (Ronald Press), 1949, the appendixes in Cleanth Brooks, *The Well Wrought Urn*, New York (Reynal and Hitchcock), 1947, and relevant sections and bibliographies in R. Wellek and A. Warren, *Theory of Literature*, New York (Harcourt Brace), 1949. It would be neither rewarding nor practicable to attach specific references to critical attitudes growing steadily more pervasive and issues growing steadily sharper, on both sides of the Atlantic, when these arise in the critical discussions which follow.

Small selected portions of the first essay below appeared in the *Kenyon Review* for 1950 (volume xii, pp. 51-75), and I wish to thank its Editors for permission to use this material here in its original and longer form. Readers interested in differing points of view regarding the value of knowledge to criticism should read Empson's courteous rejoinder, later in the same volume of that periodical, on points where I took issue with him. I decline to consider myself at war with this critic—or with 'The New Criticism', except where it asks what-is-truth? and will not stay for an answer. This book is only an attempt, within a small area, to show that criticism can be richer and truer if it will remain willing to bring all methods to bear, including those which scholarship can provide.

I wish also to thank the Clarendon Press for permission to quote Herbert's poems from F. E. Hutchinson's admirable edition of his *Works* (Oxford, 1941); to thank the Bodleian Library, the Folger Library, the Trustees of the British Museum, the Provost and Fellows of King's College, Cambridge, for permission to reproduce illustrations of works of art in their keeping; and to thank Connecticut College for a semester's leave, and for a grant in aid which assisted me with expenses incurred in the making of prints. I should express here my gratitude to the staffs of the libraries mentioned for their courtesy, had I not learned through many years' experience of that courtesy that it is a virtue above all human frailty, continuing *in saecula saeculorum* with or without gratitude; for the same reason I abstain here from thanking those who read this manuscript in whole or in part— Dorothy Bethurum, Kathleen and Geoffrey Tillotson, V. M. Couser, and Eleanor T. Lincoln. This book is not one to rouse ire in many breasts, but to enter any controversy is to rouse some, and it will exonerate these friends if I say here that they read with patience what it was too late for them to mend by advice.

ROSEMOND TUVE

CONNECTICUT COLLEGE, NEW LONDON
CONNECTICUT

July 1951

CONTENTS

TABLE OF PLATES

The most important reference to each Plate in the text of the book (Part I or II, and page) appears in italics under the indication of subject.

I wish to thank those who gave me various forms of assistance
in arranging, procuring, or choosing illustrations: Mr. Edgar
Mayhew, Mr. Geoffrey Tillotson, Mr. David Ross, and espe‑
cially Mr. David Bland and Mr. Kenneth Harrison.

PART ONE

CRITICISM, like history, must be eternally re-written. That long-suffering individual The Modern Reader is perhaps ready to interject 'but not so *often*!' He has been party to a good many rewritings.

The necessity is there, all the same. The fundamental reason for it is very familiar. The greatest work cannot stay alive without help, and even the flea can protect the mighty elephant. The flea's responsibilities in this connexion have been the subject of much discourse during the last thirty years. It is even contended by some that the elephant him-self has been all but forgotten and that the fleas are no longer keeping anyone but themselves awake, but this book declines to take that cheerless position. It will offer certain criticisms of modern critical habits of thought, in the belief that criticism of early poetry is better written when it is not separated off from the problems which vex us now, how-ever temporary they may be. Indeed this involvement with current critical problems and presuppositions is not a matter of choice for us; it can be more overt, or less. I have chosen the former. The criticism which results will need rewriting, like any other. One safeguard has been attempted: that the poet concerned should be the centre of the inquiry.

There is general though often tacit agreement on this ancillary function of criticism. As with all the humane learnings, great literature is somehow not superseded by other great literature which follows it; it retains a unique value which men are not ready to give up in the way they willingly substitute truer conceptions of how the blood cir-culates for the old ones, or new mackintoshes for the worn ones that no longer keep out the rain. Yet, though a great poem does not become untrue, or wear out, the inner core of value in it becomes obscured. It 'dies', we say; we no longer feel that pulse of life in it that made it valuable. Few would dispute the notion that the good critic pierces through to that inner core in such a way that we can see again what made a book living and valuable. And this must be done anew, and done differently, in every age.

There is general agreement on another point. Oddly enough, the critic does this revitalizing service, quite often, by making us realize that the poet's conceptions are not mistaken but true, and by giving us the grateful and excited sense that here is something which will still keep us dry in a damp world. Yet when he is finished we neither say 'How true' nor 'How useful'. We look at the poem as the Mariner looked at the water-snakes, and say 'How beautiful'. If we are not brought to this exclamation the poem is as dead as earth, and the critic may hang himself for a useless frump. Although there would be general theoretical agreement in all camps on this matter, the Modern Reader is quite right in noticing (as a great many of him does, voicing complaint) that much modern criticism does not, in fact, seem to make the poetry more pleasurable. The poem itself, to use the current language, somehow fails to become the locus of pleasure. There is pleasure, but we later uneasily realize that it is not the poem we have enjoyed. The same old modern swindle, process substituted for essence, has caught us again. 'How beautiful', we say. A beautiful point, a beautiful analysis, a beautiful instance of modern ideas glimpsed before their time, a beautiful insight into the workings of the poet's mind, a beautiful use of the Maimed God motif, a beautiful gear-shift, a beautiful paved surface, a beautiful Aga cooker, a beautiful little power lawn-mower, just the right size. How with this rage shall beauty hold a plea, whose action is no stronger than a flower?

Then there are other points on which everyone does not

agree. There are other reasons why criticism must be eternally rewritten. One of these seems to me that the areas of
human ignorance shift and change quite as much as do
human needs or human knowledge. The repairing of
ignorance used to be an accepted function for criticism. It
is possible to defend the position that great literature should
be great enough to speak to us despite our ignorance of
things the writer and his contemporaries knew, that the
burden of this lies on the poet, and that the poem should
itself bear the responsibility for making the reader a sufficiently informed reader. This book does not take that position. Conceding the fact that there are cases in which a poet
could not bridge a gap he did not envisage, I have tried
the experiment of making myself responsible as a reader for
learning what the poet seems to have expected I would
know as part of a common language.

Human knowledge grows as well as decays. Here the
problem for criticism becomes very complicated. To what
extent should we, or may we, remake literature to suit with
our new kinds of knowledge? It is part of a critic's function
to remake literature. It had been generally understood in
earlier times that he remade it only as a man reshapes an
idea to fit new needs and new possibilities of application,
not as a man remakes a block of marble into a piece of
sculpture that was only 'in it' before in a sense no sculptor
takes literally. Various critics currently writing remake
poems in this last sense, and defend this activity as a proper
function of criticism.*

This book takes the position that the second kind of

* Certain modern attitudes and controversies referred to in this book are more
characteristic of American than of British criticism. It would be both tedious
and disproportionate to make every such reference to current critical attitudes
specific, and the reader who does not recognize them as issues of considerable
prevalence and importance (and occasionally of considerable danger, or of
considerable promise) is referred to the Prefatory Note.

'making' is the artist's own province. But also the position that the first kind is possible and necessary with every work of art that ever outlasted its own tiny moment of time. That the very form and nature of literary communication, especially its use of metaphor and symbol to body forth thought, not only allows but necessitates the continual reshaping. And that the first step in thus enjoying a poem as a living event, a beautiful and true and useful thing in its own right, is to let it speak so far as possible in its own voice.

The first essay which follows is a case in point; the second is an attempt at using a method. The first is a study of a single long poem, though not without a view to the enjoyment of other writings in the same and other centuries. In the second I have tried to read many poems, but in the language they were written in, a language of images commonly understood when the poet wrote, believing that the poetry would thus have the beauty and life its creator gave it, but that it would also *thus* translate itself, as all metaphors do, into significances potent here and now.

The major purpose of all this is not to study or to illustrate critical theories, but to read Herbert. In all careful reading, however, a theory of criticism is either implicitly or overt, and the first essay concerns itself explicitly with modern criticism, for it tries to put into practice many ideas denied in the best (or at least the most vigorous) of that criticism. Notably it tries to put into practice the idea that a poem is most beautiful and most meaningful to us when it is read in terms of the tradition which gave it birth. Since modern criticism at its best is brilliant, conscientious, and full of promise, I have thought it proper to proceed in the first essay on both fronts simultaneously, not only reading Herbert's 'The Sacrifice' in my own way but openly examining the most important single modern study of a Herbert poem, William Empson's critique of the piece by that title.

Empson gave some nine pages to a treatment of 'The Sacrifice' as an example of the seventh of his *Seven Types of Ambiguity*. These pages, through brilliant exposition of meanings apparent and hidden, bring a reader closer to the heart and core of a beautiful poem than much criticism of Herbert between his day and our own has been able to do. They also demonstrate certain undeniable virtues of modern criticism, and the skilful use of its most typical instruments, especially of those provided for a critic's use by various developments of modern psychology. Nevertheless, a reader familiar with the traditions out of which this poem sprang will find Empson's reading inadequate. This essay is concerned to supply these felt deficiencies of interpretation. Simultaneously it will attempt to examine the problems which are raised by the use of certain favoured instruments or methods in much modern criticism, and by its ignoring of various others.

The type of ambiguity which 'The Sacrifice' is said to exemplify is that type wherein two opposite meanings are defined by the context, 'so that the total effect is to show a fundamental division in the writer's mind'.[1] Empson speaks of the poem as an example 'where the contradictory impulses that are held in equilibrium by the doctrine of atonement may be seen in a luminous juxtaposition', and analyses various stanzas to demonstrate how 'only the speed, isolation, and compactness *of Herbert's method* could handle in this way impulses of such reach and complexity' (my italics).

To my mind also this is a great and original poem. But in point of fact it is a reminder to us that a poem is irremediably implicated in its past, and we shall even as a sort of

[1] *Seven Types of Ambiguity*, London (Chatto and Windus), 1930, p. 244; the treatment of this particular poem is at pp. 284 ff. Quotations from Herbert's poem are from F. E. Hutchinson's edition of his *Works*, Oxford (Clarendon Press), 1941, pp. 26–34; my references are to line numbers.

by-point have to reconsider what we can possibly mean by 'originality'. It is useful to look at a poem as if it had no past, as much modern criticism so well and so pugna-ciously does. But other ways of looking are necessary if we wish to see it, and these other ways are especially necessary the moment we make the most innocent remark about the writer's 'mind' or the poet's 'method'. This particular poem's basic invention or structural situation, the sequence of ironies upon which it is built, the occurrence, setting, and application of the refrain which bind it together, the very collocation of the antitheses which make it up, are none of them Herbert's.

Herbert's poem belongs with two interlinked groups, both well known, of medieval lyrics; both groups belong as does his poem to a larger group, the Complaints of Christ to His People. All possibly had their spring in the liturgical offices of Holy Week, most obviously (for one group) in the *Improperia* or Reproaches of Good Friday.[2] The particular ironies which Herbert uses with greatest effect towards the end of the poem have had their widest currency by reason of the use of the *Improperia* in the *Adora-tio Crucis*, on that day; the earlier poems in the tradition of which Herbert's is a part make use (as he probably does) of the sequence of responsories for Matins of Maundy Thurs-day, Good Friday, and Holy Saturday. This sequence had made traditional, in music and in vernacular lyric, the application Herbert makes of the O *vos omnes qui transitis*: 'O all ye who passe by, behold and see . . . Was ever grief like mine?' Some of the loveliest polyphonic music of the late sixteenth and early seventeenth centuries—some

---

[2] Rosemary Freeman notices that this poem is related to the *Improperia* in a note in her *English Emblem Books*, London, 1948, p. 162. That we had each remarked upon this we discovered in a conversation in 1948, when her book was in proof and this present essay long since completed. Neither Canon Hutchinson's notes nor any critics of Herbert notice these liturgical connexions.

perhaps which moved him most on those twice-a-week journeys to Salisbury Cathedral when Walton tells us he 'would usually sing and play his part at an appointed private Music-meeting'—was written for these liturgical uses, and preserves in a form more moving than any other those ironic contrasts which the liturgy, not Herbert, had put into Christ's mouth. This paragraph notes only the first and most striking point of relationship with a pervasive tradition (familiar in the graphic arts, other literary genres, other writings) which we shall presently examine with more care.

I do not know whether it makes an extreme difference to what Empson most wished to bring out that the 'method' is not 'Herbert's method', that the luminous juxtaposition is equally not his. It may. He says of Herbert's poem that 'the various sets of conflicts in the Christian doctrine of the Sacrifice are stated with an assured and easy simplicity, a reliable and unassuming grandeur, extraordinary in any material, but *unique as achieved by successive fireworks of contra-diction, and a mind jumping like a flea*'. When we realize that the assured simplicity and the unassuming grandeur had accompanied the statement of these conflicts for some hundreds of years, the word 'unique' pulls us up with some sharpness, for of course successive fireworks of con-tradiction very like these had been set off in public and to all men's eyes and ears for generations, and Herbert's mind makes its jumps under the very precise guidance of those who had made the jumps before him. But there are two points here, and they are interesting for the theory of criticism.

The first is this point of dependence. The ironies in Herbert's poem are no less marvellous for speed and com-pactness because they were found by others; the tone, 'the strange monotony of accent', is no less fitting because it is also the tone of the Reproaches and of sundry medieval lyrics; we must note and praise these excellences quite aside from any knowledge of their being conventions rather than inventions of this poet. But can we construct notions of what *is* 'Herbert's method' while regarding such knowledge as impertinent? (To the *act* of decision concerning aesthetic value the knowledge seems to me impertinent. Nevertheless, it assists—and sometimes even provides—the state of awareness whence such decisions arise.) But do we somehow phrase our criticism differently, when we realize that the 'achievement' by which 'all these references are brought together' (Empson, p. 293) and 'kept in their frame, of monotonous and rather naïve pathos' happens not to be Herbert's achievement? and that the same 'rarefied intensity of feeling' characterizes many moving and beautiful Middle English poems which use this same frame? The danger may enter especially when we imperceptibly move from remarks about the poem to remarks about the poet's style or achievement; but *if we think we can avoid so moving,* I believe we deceive ourselves. How can we know the dancer from the dance? It may be that criticism of 'the poem as poem' requires a division between creation and creator which is not possible because of the nature of 'meaning' in language. It is time we recognize this impossibility if it exists. It may be, also, that we have no choice but to keep trying to do this impossible thing. But then we had best be openminded rather than arrogant about relating a poem's genesis to its meaning. Many modern critics, trying to separate criticism from 'scholarship', are inclined to a certain pugnacious arrogance in this respect.

But there is another and more teasing point. Language is a social phenomenon and no man's private oyster, so that there is such a thing as misreading; and meanings have histories, and shrink as well as expand, so that there is such

a thing as ignorance of one's misreadings. Hence it is that—
little as modern criticism cares to acknowledge it—meanings of elements or motifs in poems, like meanings of single
words, are clarified by knowledge of meanings those elements have carried before the poem was written, and as we
think 'outside' it. Much that is 'outside' a poem to us was
well inside it to our forefathers, and still is to some readers.

I speak here rather of our typical modern presuppositions
than of Empson, but, for an example, there are various
cases in which his readings of this poem are pretty well
ruled out, as too limited, by such knowledge. Christ says
in Herbert's poem (121):

> Why, Caesar is their onely King, not I:
> He clave the stonie rock, when they were drie;
> But surely not their hearts, as I well trie:
> > Was ever grief like mine?

Empson thinks of this as Christ identifying 'Caesar with
Moses as the chosen leader of Israel' in the bitterness of his
'apology' or 'defence'. But it is next to impossible to think
of it thus narrowly if one is conscious of the liturgical and
patristic identification of Moses with Christ, of the legendary and iconographical identification of Moses' rod with
the wood of the Cross, and if there rings in one's ears the
sorrowful but accusatory contrast of the Good Friday
Reproaches:

> I gave thee to drink wholesome water [*aqua salutis*] from the rock:
> > and thou hast given me gall and vinegar.
> O *my people*,* what have I done to thee? or in what have I
> > afflicted thee?

> * *Popule meus, quid feci tibi*, and from this phrase known as the *Popule meus*.

'Cleaving the stony rock' is far more than a mere allusion
to Moses the chosen leader. No cleric of the seventeenth

century, as liturgically literate as George Herbert, and brought up on typology, could mention this act of Moses without thinking both of the water from the side of Christ, the living rock (as in Herbert, 170), and of the mystical regenerative power of water, so stressed, for example, in the services for Easter Even. The connexions ultimately, of course, are with the culture-hero who gave his people life-giving water in the wilderness of the dry rock, the land waste through guilt; and the primitive depth of such mean-ings would be in some sort present to a seventeenth-century Christian who read, 'I, Christ, gave thee to drink of the healing water, I am all Saviours, and Moses was I. *Caesar* your King and regenerator! Alas, he cannot cleave those hearts of stone which make you scourge Me, those hearts which I as just judge must sometime punish—was ever grief like Mine?' One of the multiple ironic implications of 'King' is, of course, present as well in the 'We have no king but Caesar' passage in John xix. 15, the Gospel for the same day (Good Friday). They spoke truly, had no regenerating King, but they knew not what they said; Herbert's line cries out to be read as a terrible and damning irony rather than as Empson's 'I am not a political agitator'.

Whole stanzas of Herbert's poem gain their compressed force from that acceptance of Moses as a type of Christ which is a commonplace of iconography, of other Holy Week offices, of Christian literature of all types.[3] This typological parallel, especially the specific element in it used in the stanza quoted, was *within not outside* the poem to Herbert and his generation. This is not only because it had been a commonplace of biblical commentary for centuries,

[3] If we wish to span a whole period with one reference, the much-read and much-edited Prudentius, and Erasmus his commentator, discourse on it (see the 16th- and 17th-century editions; the Christmas and Epiphany hymns, *Cathemerinon* xi and xii). Prudentius was set as a school text. See the Note on accessibility of these materials to the 17th-century reader, at the end of this book.

but because the rock struck by Moses is allegorized as referring to Christ in 1 Cor. x. 4, and because it is one of the commonest of all iconographical symbols of the sacra⁄ments issuing from the side of Christ the living rock. I do not wish to interrupt the argument here to make citations. But to anyone familiar with illustrated books of the Renais⁄sance the piercing of Christ's side becomes almost synony⁄mous with Moses' striking of the rock to bring forth the stream of saving water, merely through familiarity with the parallel vignettes of those scenes in the *Biblia Pauperum* and in the margins of illustrated Books of Hours (see Plates II, III *a*; the first⁄named was so popular as to be virtually a handbook of iconographical convention—e.g. for the windows of King's College, Cambridge). It had become a commonplace of sacred poetry at least as early as Pru⁄dentius's famous hymn, the *Inventor rutili dux bone luminis*, where both the struck rock and the bitter waters converted into water sweet as honey are related to that 'lignum', the Cross, which changes bitterness into sweetness.[4]

Caesar clave the stony Rock; quite true. It is not Caesar who can cleave the rock; also quite true. The line has two explicit, stated, unambiguous (in the commonest sense) meanings, besides the implied and suggested ones. The terror in Herbert's lines depends from our realizing the enormity of an error which confuses the Caesars of the world with the eternal regenerative King, and from our perceiving the fearful ineluctable connexion between this error and Christ's kingly function as Judge. The sacrificial 'mysteriousnesse' to which Christ's grief is 'wound up' (next stanza) is attached at one end to an 'identification' of

[4] See *Cathem.* v. 89 ff. Herbert's reference to the stream of blood issuing from the side of a great rock in 'Love unknown', p. 129, is in this tradition, and uses others. For the illustrated books mentioned see the Note on accessibility just referred to, and see the more detailed treatments of such books in Part II below, where iconographical relations are more carefully pursued.

Caesar far more blindly mistaken than that Empson sees,
and at the other end to Herbert's continuation:

> They buffet him, and box him as they list,
> Who grasps the earth and heaven with his fist,
> And never yet, whom he would punish, miss'd:
> 　　　　　Was ever grief like mine?

The combination of irony and pity with inescapably just
judgement makes for a 'concentration' yet more 'powerful'
than that which Empson remarked. The threat of Judgement is a familiar element in Complaint of Christ poems.[5]
And the typological identification of Christ with Moses—
common to all the materials Herbert echoes—was assuredly
in the author's mind, if that makes any odds to our reading.
If it does not make any odds, I submit that we are stubborn
readers. Better even to be accused of that new critical sin
the Intentional Fallacy than thus to accede to Wisdom-
at-one-entrance-quite-shut-out.

Again, one of Herbert's most striking antitheses reads:

> *O all ye who passe by, behold and see;*
> Man stole the fruit, but I must climbe the tree;
> The tree of life to all, but onely me:
> 　　　　　Was ever grief like mine?　　　(201)

I shall presently treat this stanza in considerable detail for
other reasons, but one question it brings up is relevant here.
'He climbs the tree to repay what was stolen, as if he was
putting the apple back', says Empson, later commenting

---

[5] Christ may say in a similar context: 'All this world is in my hand; ven-
geance I may take where it please me, on water or land' (xv: 107); 'I can make
the earth to shake' (EETS 124, p. 46). For convenience in quoting rapidly
from many pieces I have adopted xiii: 100, xiv: 100, and xv: 100 as conventional
references to numbered lyrics in Carleton Brown's three volumes of 13th-, 14th-,
and 15th-century *Religious Lyrics*, and I give merely the volume and page of
various Early English Text Society collections used, furnishing full titles and
other data in the Note on conventions used in quoting, at the end of this book.

that this makes Christ smaller, more childlike, than Eve, who could reach the apple without climbing; 'but the *phrase in itself implies rather* that he is doing the stealing'. Does it imply this? Perhaps a critic has to decide whether or not it makes any difference to us that it could not have implied this to Herbert (in so far as there is certainty in mortal affairs), that the phrase about climbing the tree (ascending the Cross) is the veriest commonplace, and that the antithetical pairing of the two trees is used with mean⁄ings that would be yet more germane to Herbert's poem, in sequence and in vernacular lyric, in antiphon and *com⁄munio*, in the oft⁄published Meditations on the Passion of pseudo⁄Augustine, in apocryphal gospel and *Golden Legend*, in the *Crux benedicta* and the *Crux fidelis*, in all those liturgical materials which the remainder of his poem echoes so persistently. Actually, there is no such thing as 'the phrase in itself'. The locution marks a modern critical error, and philology should have taught us all to be wary of it. 'The son stealing from his father's orchard is a symbol of incest', says Empson; 'Jesus seems a child in this meta⁄phor'. But to whom? Perhaps it is the answer to this last question which every critic has a responsibility to make clear. It is not possible to read the many, many uses of this liturgically common contrast and think that Jesus seems a child or an apple⁄stealer in them—if words, tone, context, can convey anything at all trustworthy to us ever; nor is it possible then to read Herbert and feel that his use differs from these others in words or tone or context. This reserva⁄tion seems to me relevant to one's way of reading the poem, certainly to a study of what '*Herbert* deals with' (Empson, p. 295) in it.

On the other hand, the reservation does not seem relevant if a critic merely wishes to discover what a poem can mean to him, can become under his hands. This is a valuable

activity, and it is only too bad that it is generally accompanied by implications that this meaning is 'the meaning',
and that one may praise the (original) author for it. One
should praise rather the critic, who is the author of another
and different poem—and why should he not be? The more
good poems in the world the better. But he should acknowledge his paternity. I do not take up the problem (clearest
in modern strictures on Spenser) offered by the fact that
we are oftener asked to condemn than to admire these out-
of-wedlock late-born waifs. And their supposed but long-
dead 'fathers' too. A horrid hent.

I shall not venture farther in the rest of this essay into the
question of what-the-poem-'really'-means; there is a bog of
subjectivity just to one side in the darkness, and I would
rather leave the skirting of it to others. I am frankly interested
in what Herbert meant. The reasons for this interest are
neither psychological nor historical; the chief one is that
I have learned to trust Herbert's aesthetic judgement. 'The
Sacrifice' is a beautiful poem, read in any of the ways men
have read it. But read by the illumination of the tradition
in which it was conceived it takes on a richness, a depth,
complexity, and moving power which I am loath to go
without just because I do not know the things Herbert
knew until I study them out.

Two well-known poetic and liturgical traditions, joined
before Herbert joined them, meet to make the initial 'invention' without which there would be no poem. The first,
the extra-scriptural Monologue or Complaint of Christ,
which provides the formal basis and thence exerts much
influence upon the tone, became a poetic convention as
early as we have extant religious lyrics in Middle English.
It appears before that in Latin and in Old English, for
example in Cynewulf's *Christ* and in sermons. The
medieval lyrics in this kind are often very lovely, especially

II. *Biblia Pauperum*, block-book, B.Mus.: Eve's creation, Side-wound, Moses and rock

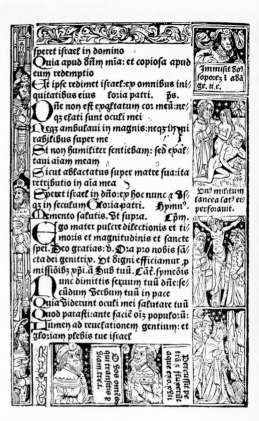

III *a. Horae,* 1488/9 (Dupré):
Eve's creation, Side-wound,
Moses and rock

III *b. Bible moral.,* B.Mus. MS.
Addit. 18719, f. 3ᵛ, xiii *c.*:
Eve's creation, Side-wound

metrically, and are oftenest emotionally powerful because they are appeals to man, and emphasize Christ's sorrows as earnest of a love which asks only man's love in return. The motif of ingratitude or 'unkindness' is not seldom intro׳ duced, carrying with it details of the Passion (as in Her׳ bert), and the element of wry contrast often goes to the length of compressed 'witty' antitheses:

> Thyn hondes streite gloued,
> white & clene kept;
> Myne with nailes thorled,
> on rode. . . .
>
> (xiv: 126)[6]

The use of witty conceits or turns of speech is no more thought to be outside the tone deemed proper for this situa׳ tion than Herbert thought it; Christ rides his 'steed' or 'palfrey', the Cross, 'in red array'; his skin is the parchment on which our charter of salvation is written. A variant of the Monologue of Christ, the Dialogue between Jesus and the Virgin at the Cross, may have a Mary who says 'now on the rood is made *thy nest*', and a Christ who replies,

> On rode i hange for mannis sake,
> This gamen alone me must pleyye.
>
> (xiv: 67)

Herbert's supposedly Metaphysical harshness or irony in the diction is quite native to the tradition.

One group of these monologues is formed by the *O vos omnes qui transitis* poems. Christ's first words, as in Herbert, will be some variant of these phrases from Lam. i. 12, where, of course, they are said by the city of Jerusalem. They are twice repeated, as if by Christ, in the Good

---

[6] Other contrasts are, thy garland: my thorns; thy fashionable slit robe: my opened side. The two references immediately following are to poems in the Vernon MS., the second a 'Testament of Christ' piece (EETS 117, pp. 626, 637).

Friday and Holy Saturday responsories, and it is liturgical convention, not Herbert, which makes 'any grief like unto my grief' apply to *Christ's* sorrow. Even the Croxton Miracle Play of the Sacrament makes Christ's 'image' speak these words to the blasphemous Jews who have pricked the Host. In lyrics, Christ's complaint may begin 'Ye that pasen be the weyye,   Abidet a litel stounde!' (xiv: 74); 'Thow synfull man that by me gais,   Ane quhyle to me thou turne thi face!' (xv: 102); 'Brother, a⁄byde, . . . A⁄byde, a⁄byde and here thy brother speke' (xv: 109).

Both in liturgy and in lyric the conventionalizing of a situation, for one thing, fixes certain words and ideas inex⁄ tricably in a particular frame of reference—as the 'attendite, et videte Si est dolor similis sicut dolor meus' become inescapably Christ's own words, for Herbert or for Handel, so that we must be chary of interpretations based on a lively sense of their being rather said by the city of Jerusalem 'in the original'. Compare here Empson's discussion—yet he rightly and acutely sees that a possible double reference would be somehow related to Christ's later 'Weep not . . . Your tears for your own fortunes should be kept'; He has wept for both (149). Herbert's 'original' was not a verse in Lamentations, but a well⁄known and effortlessly accepted tradition which made a double reference to both Old and New Testament, with all the resulting implications, abso⁄ lutely inescapable. Christ both is and weeps for His people; the grief is both cause and remedy. These portions of Lamentations had been read on the last three days of Holy Week in Sarum Use for hundreds of years; this is probably why Donne put them into verse. Christ's weeping over the 'razing' of Jerusalem—both the temporal downfall and the ultimate spiritual death of His people—had been for cen⁄ turies thought of as prefigured by Jeremiah's weeping over the destruction of Jerusalem, and by Isaiah's.

The three of them weep, in paralleled vignettes, in the popular iconographical series mentioned a few pages above (in the *Biblia Pauperum*, and the margins of very many illustrated *Hours* and Books of Christian Prayer; see Plate V *a*), and also in the widely translated *Speculum humanae salvationis*. 'This weeping of our Lord Christ was some/ time figuratively showed in the lamentations of the prophet Jeremy', says the *Speculum*; treatises on the church year, like Durandus's, treat Jeremiah's lament for Jerusalem's fall under Palm Sunday.[7] The tears of Jeremiah, of Christ entering Jerusalem, of Christ at Gethsemane when His 'friends' could not wake with Him one hour, of the daughters of Jerusalem to whom Christ (bearing His Cross) said the 'weep not' quoted by Herbert—these were all one stream, and to both Herbert and his readers the lament penned by Jeremiah was not only fitly but inevitably Christ's own utterance: 'O all ye who pass by. . . . Was ever grief like mine?'

But besides this fixing of certain words in an accepted frame of reference, something else happens—very important for poetry—when convention telescopes several different actual happenings into one symbolic situation or speech. The *oratio* of Christ is abstracted from the world of histori/ cal events; it does not take place in a particular space or time; as in Herbert, parts of it are delivered as from the Cross, yet the *now* of stanza 2 or 9 is much earlier; tenses vary, and there is no sense of a narrative being actually told; Christ seems to be still saying these things and still weeping

---

[7] Part II below describes the *Speculum*, an important repository of icono/ graphical conventions, and the illustrated series of 'Queen Elizabeth's Prayer/ books'. For all these and for Durandus see the Note on accessibility of these materials, at the end of this book. Interesting confirmation of the popularity of the *O vos omnes* is the fact that this is the legend chosen by Claus Sluter for Jere/ miah's sculptured scroll, in his famous Puits de Moïse (C. R. Morey, *Mediaeval Art*, pp. 355–6).

over 'Jerusalem', nor do we listen to what He says with an ear alert to verisimilitude or to the psychological consistency of a speaking 'character'. This has already happened in the fourteenth-century uses of the convention; 'Abyde, gud men' (xiv: 46) is written in an eternal present:

> Bihald thi self the soth, & se
> How I am hynged here on this tre
>   And nayled fute & hand.

The Middle Ages were more thoroughly aware than we that poetry has quite as much kinship with ritual as with drama, that poetic immediacy comes as well through time-lessness as through vividness.

Both liturgical and poetic tradition frequently emphasize the irony of the gap between Christ's actual omnipotent power and the specific indignities He suffers, conceiving of Him (as does Herbert) as the Jehovah of the Exodus, as First Cause and Creator—so that anything else *but* the equation between 'I' and 'the Deitie', which Empson takes note of, would be unthinkable. 'I am he that made the erth, water and fire', says Christ (xv: 103; cf. Herbert, 67: 'he that built the world'). 'Pepyll that passe me by', says Christ in the Towneley Crucifixion play, 'I made thee in my likeness'. 'I made thee in my image', or 'I made all beasts bow to thee; I gave thee free will', are frequent sources of ironic contrast in the various Complaint of Christ poems.[8]

Despite these hints of unused power, the usual emphasis or tone in these Complaints may be signalized in the words which mark off another grouping within the kind: 'Homo vide quid pro te patior.' The Latin lines of Philippe de Grève (d. 1236) which thus begin, their Anglo-Norman

---

[8] These three may be found in EETS (extra ser.) 71, vv. 233 ff.; EETS 124, pp. 85 ff.; EETS 15, pp. 198 ff. Concerning the *Homo vide* group next mentioned, see Carleton Brown's notes, and typical texts, xiv: 70, 77.

and English counterparts, many lyrics, many hymns, all are
first and foremost songs by Christ of love for man. If we
did not willingly recognize this emphasis upon 'my tender-
nesse' (Herbert, 125) and its relation to the uniqueness of
Christ's grief, in Herbert's particular version of the *O vos
omnes qui transitis* tradition, we should much mistake the
tone of many of his uses of the refrain.

The ironies are much sharper, the antitheses much neater,
and the double meanings emphasized by Herbert more
clear and terrible, in the second more narrow and definite
tradition—the *Improperia* (Reproaches) of Good Friday. It
is convenient to term this tradition the *Popule meus*, from
the first words spoken; they come to be thought of as overtly
spoken, dramatically rather than ritualistically, by Christ
in His own person. The liturgical tradition entered medieval
vernacular lyric to produce some of the most beautiful of
Middle English poems—laconic, powerful, and terse with
the understatements borrowed from the liturgical text. The
portion of this Good Friday office which most interests us
consists of a series of brief and sardonic contrasts, sung by
two cantors (as it were the words of Christ), to each of
which the deacons or choir respond with the Trisagion, or
threefold Sanctus in Greek. For example:

> Because I led thee through the wilderness forty years, and I
> fed thee with manna, and brought thee into a land
> sufficiently good, thou hast prepared a cross for thy
> Saviour.

> Agyos O Theos, Agyos Iskyros, &c.

> What could I have done more unto thee that I have not
> done? I planted thee indeed, O my vineyard, with fair
> fruit, and thou art become very bitter unto me; for thou
> gavest me to drink in my thirst vinegar mingled with
> gall, and piercedst thy Saviour's side with a spear.

Agyos O Theos, Agyos Iskyros, &c.

(*Sarum Missal in English*, tr. F. E. Warren, i. 258)

In the laconic contrasts of Herbert's Reproaches of Christ, as in those of the medieval lyrics, sound the echoes of the Reproaches sung during many centuries of Good Fridays:

> They give me vineger mingled with gall,
> But more with malice: yet, when they did call,
> With Manna, Angels food, I fed them all:
> > Was ever grief like mine?
>
> Then on my head a crown of thorns I wear:
> For these are all the grapes *Sion* doth bear,
> Though I my vine planted and watred there:
> > Was ever grief like mine?

> > > > (Herbert, 237, 161)

> Fourti wenter i sente the
> angeles mete fro heuene;
> & thu heng me on rode tre,
> & greddist with loud steuene.   (cried; voice)
>
> Heilsum water i sente the
> out of the harde ston;
> & eysil & galle thu sentist me,
> other gef thu me non.
>
> I made thin enemies & the
> for to ben knowen o∕sunder;
> & on an hey hil thu henge me,
> al the werld on me to wonder.   (xiv: 72)

Ich the vedde and shrudde the;   (fed and clothed)
And thou wyth eysyl drinkest to me, (vinegar)
And wyth spere styngest me.
> My volk, what habbe y do the?

In bem of cloude ich ladde the;
And to pylate thou ledest me.
> My volk, what habbe y do the?

Of the ston ich dronk to the;
And thou wyth galle drincst to me.
My volk, what habbe y do the?

Ich yaf the croune of kynedom;
And thou me yifst a croune of thorn.
My volk, what habbe y do the?

(xiv: 15; by another 'Herebert', d. 1333)

The vinegar as a kind of toast which 'thou drinkest to me'
is typical of what happens in this tradition, and long before
Herbert used it. The *Popule meus* which forms the refrain
after each of the thirteen stanzas of the last-quoted poem no
doubt reflects the use of this versicle ('Popule meus, quid
feci tibi? aut in quo contristavi te? responde mihi') as a
responsory sung by both choirs after a second series of
stinging antitheses, in the liturgy. The cantors of the two
choirs sing antiphonally: what more should I have done?
I led you out of Egypt, drowning Pharaoh, you sell me to
princes; with angels' meat I fed you, you buffet me; I struck
down the kings of Canaan, you strike my head (cf. xiv: 72
with the modern *Liber usualis*). The parallels with Christ
were widely emphasized iconographically; for manna:
Eucharist see Plates IV, X *b*, XIV, XV, and for Red Sea
delivery: Baptism see V *b*, VI. Since flexibility of length
was necessary to provide for differing numbers of persons
venerating the Cross, and so on, various antiphons and
hymns were used, including consistently Venantius Fortunatus' *Crux fidelis* with its parallel between the 'first tree'
and Christ's *arbor nobilis*, of which I shall have more to say
later. The famous *Liber sacerdotalis* of 1523[9] prescribes the

---

[9] See Karl Young, *Drama of the Medieval Church* (Oxford, 1933); students
interested in relations of the *Adoratio crucis* (and the *Improperia*) to the drama will
find material especially at i. 117 ff., 493 ff. A good example of late use of the
Popule meus tradition is D. Heinsius's Passion homily, tr. by I. Harmer, 1618
(*Mirrour of Humilitie*, STC 13039), where the refrain introduces many pages

use of that Good Friday and Holy Saturday Matins re-
sponsory which contains Herbert's refrain, and his *incipit*:
'Videte omnes populi, Si est dolor similis sicut dolor meus.
O vos omnes, qui transitis per viam, attendite et videte.'

With so little of any of these texts before our eyes, I shall
not pause now to demonstrate how a similarity of formal
basis, initial situation, and thence of poetic feeling has produced a similarity of tone in the liturgical, the medieval,
and the Herbert 'reproaches', written though they were
centuries apart and showing plenty of verbal independence.
It would be especially tempting to remark the Yeats-like,
ritualistic, modal changes in an identical refrain when it
occurs in differing contexts (an effect found in various
medieval poems as well as in Herbert's). Or to demonstrate
the effect of the basic structure provided by the liturgical
text—flat, unelaborated statements of antitheses generally
found from one like verb or noun. Or to study the curious
mingling of hardness with pathos, metrically conveyed
(quite independently, of course) in the Herbert and the
Middle English poems. The patient, considering, accusatory rise and fall of 'Othĕr ǵef thŭ m̂e ńon' is precisely
similar to the tone, especially in the final cadence, of many
lines in Herbert: 'The tree of life to all, but onely me', 'My
face they cover, though it be divine'. The feminine rhyme
forces a hint of irony into the voice in lines apropos the
mocking crowd—'al the werld on me to wonder', cf. Herbert, 141, 'Servants and abjects flout me; they are wittie:
Now prophesie who strikes thee, is their dittie.' Many such

given to the typical contrasts: the author of liberty led captive; yet I made thee,
of dust; you have slain him that brought you out of the land of Egypt; slain him
that fed you in the wilderness with the bread of angels. Antitheses produce the
usual effect upon the tone: I looked for amity, found enmity. Or, of the vine of
Sion, 'wherefore when I looked it should have brought foorth grapes, brought
it foorth thornes, with which now the Temples of my head are wounded?'; I
looked for wine, it brought forth vinegar.

minute but fascinating similarities are due simply to simi-larities in *genre* and inspiration. But one more general point, which does not depend on such careful textual comparison, should be made.

The tension of ambiguities and serried meanings which Empson has commented on is precisely what Herbert owes to the tradition, and it is our appreciation of these which is deepened by a knowledge of what he built upon. Herbert's poem is full of minute shocks, of unexpected connexions, sudden recoils in the emotion described or produced—and it is this temper or tone, along with the ironic contrasts which usually bring the shock to bear, which he inherited. His is not the Christ we know in Luke's or Matthew's straightforward narrative—but He *is* the Christ of the liturgy of Holy Week. The importance of the sacrificial idea with its reach into primitive levels of feeling, the almost savage implications of impending retribution, the profound doublenesses of meaning which will not yield to a recon-ciliation except at the heart of the Mystery—these are what Herbert found ready to his hand. For the most part, these inhere in no single statement in the liturgical text proper, any more than they do in Herbert, but if one wishes to analyse latent ambiguities, there is quite enough to occupy one in the *because* (*quia*) and the merged identities of

Because I brought thee up out of the land of Egypt, thou hast prepared a cross for thy Saviour.

Because I led thee through the wilderness forty years, and I fed thee with manna, . . . thou has prepared a cross for thy Saviour.

Before thee I opened the sea, and thou hast opened my side with a spear.

O my people, what have I done to thee . . .

And Herbert's double meanings in the ambiguous 'Was ever grief like mine' toll forth the same fearful accusation as

the 'parasti crucem Salvatori tuo . . . parasti crucem Salvatori tuo . . . Popule meus . . .' of Christ's Good Friday
indictment of man, wedding the questions of the apocryphal IV Esdras of the Old Testament to the Passion of
the New.

It is my judgement that deliberate borrowing is involved,
and were that the primary interest of this essay this would
perhaps be the place to draw the noose tight. I am concerned mostly, however, with the relation between a given
seventeenth-century religious poem and a very widely diffused tradition, and with the problems which such relations
raise for criticism. It is important to recall these problems
at points where their specific connexion with a 'good'
reading of particular poems can become apparent. One
problem is that of our ignorance. For however apparent
these relations may seem when someone has pointed them
out, neither annotation nor criticism of Herbert takes
account of them (no more does criticism of many another
seventeenth-century poet, or many a definition of 'the baroque' or of 'Metaphysical wit'). What kind of readers do
we make, whom circumstances have intervened to make
ignorant of what every literate man once knew? Herein lies
one of the most unfortunate effects of the wilful modern
divorce between 'scholarship' and 'criticism'. I should like
to speak out for willingness to repair our ignorances, despite
the current fear (not least current among 'academic' critics)
that we may somehow substitute knowledge 'about' poem
and author for response to poetry. This *substitution*, which
I admit to be deplorable, is far less frequent than the losses
we sustain by the modern necessity to avoid any noticeable
use of the helps furnished by literary scholarship *in case
criticism is one's end*. Revolt against the abuses of the former
may have been necessary. But criticism may not longer decline to face the problems created by the fact that recogni-

tion of the richest and deepest meanings of poems sometimes depends about equally upon the knowledge and upon the sensibility of a reader. The fact operates as truly in the case of early poems as with those of Eliot or Yeats; there it has been recognized and valiantly met.

A critic's responsibility to be knowledgeable depends a good deal perhaps on how widely diffused any given kind of knowledge once was. I have been speaking as if the tradition here dealt with, in its branching forms, were only to be met with in the Sarum Missal and in the collections of medieval lyrics with which Carleton Brown's scholarship has provided us. This of course is not true. It found its way into the drama of the guilds; thirteen stanzas of a 'Dolorous Complaint' of Christ on the Cross, an Oallyewhopassby poem (xv: 102) were incorporated into the Towneley Resurrection play; another example occurs in the Crucifixion of the same cycle, and Chester, York, and Coventry all show the influence of the tradition.[10] In less strict form it found its way into sermons; a powerful variant is the accusing Christ of the Judgement Day (in poems as well, as in the 'Fifteen Signs of Doomsday'). A Good Friday sermon of Bishop Fisher's uses the Christour charter convention (His wounds the letters written on the parchment), quotes the 'All ye who pass by' as Christ's complaint, and piles up ten or twelve paradoxes similar to Herbert's: the powerful One bound, author of liberty roped up, &c. Ten lines of related verse are put into Christ's mouth in the Good Friday sermon of the *Speculum Sacerdotale*,

[10] This was noticed long ago by G. C. Taylor in an article on 'The Relation of the English Corpus Christi Play to the M. E. Religious Lyric' (*MP*, v [1907], esp. p. 8 and note); there is even some possibility (treated by both Young and Chambers) that this *planctus Christi* was the germ of the passion plays. The 'Fifteen Signs', and the sermon references which follow, may be found in: EETS 24, pp. 124 ff.; EETS extra ser. 27, pp. 388 ff.; EETS 200, pp. 112-13; EETS extra ser. 96, p. 113. Such works utilize widely known Latin sources.

a collection arranged according to the church year. Mirk's similar collection the *Festial*, of which there were many fifteenth- and early sixteenth-century editions, ascribes to St. Bernard a Christ's Complaint in the Passion Sunday homily; its series of brittle contrasts found their way from the same source no doubt into a fourteenth-century lyric: thou hast a garland, I have a crown of thorns; thou white gloves, I bloody hands; thou spreadest thine arms in the dance, I mine on the cross (xiv: 126). Mirk's explanations of the symbolic purport of Holy Week ceremonies, including the Holy Saturday procession to the font—which is as usual identified with the Red Sea, wherein all our sins are drowned—remind us that even the considerably later audience of Herbert's poem was schooled to think in symbols, and did not interpret as flatly as we do his

> Without me each one, who doth now me brave,
> Had to this day been an Egyptian slave. (9)

Now as in Herbert's time, music is a route by which many persons not otherwise familiar with liturgy or medieval literature become familiar with traditions like the *Popule meus*; Palestrina's poignant Reproaches have been sung every Good Friday since the 1560's and '70's in the Sistine chapel, and his and Vittoria's were surely heard and sung by non-Puritan Englishmen as often as among us; there are beautiful settings for the Holy Thursday, Good Friday, and Holy Saturday responsories. The tradition was carried and spread in Latin hymns; anyone who likes may read in Drêves' *Analecta Hymnica* (xxxi. 58) an address of Christ's to man which begins like Herbert's 'O vos omnes, qui transitis', which elaborates on the outcast-God concept and stresses at once the outrageousness and the necessity of the 'rex immensus . . . in crucem extensus, pro peccatis populi'. More famous hymns like those of Prudentius or Venantius

Fortunatus (showing connexions we shall notice) were read as part of the corpus of Christian Latin poetry for their literary worth. The vast literature of anonymous (or attributed) hymns, Latin and vernacular treatments of the Passion, legendary amplifications, iconography, Biblical commentary, all fed into the stream of devotional literature endlessly reprinted in the sixteenth and seventeenth centuries. We shall see connexions with the protestantized and much translated and reprinted 'meditations' ascribed to Augustine, and with 'Anselm's' and with 'Bernard's'; the Primers based on the *Horae Beatae Mariae* so commonly owned by the laity remained popular; and, of course, all old service books did not automatically disappear, nor all medieval lyrics remain unprinted (cf. Lydgate's *Testament*, or the *Popule meus* poem, xv: 105, printed by Copland). Nor need we think that men who commonly read blackletter were frightened off by a fifteenthcentury hand; and plenty of these poems occur in Cambridge manuscripts, various ones in manuscripts of Herbert's own college. Since 'The Sacrifice' is the second poem in that section titled 'The Church' in Herbert's volume, it would be a pleasure to think that he saw a Jesus College, Cambridge, manuscript in which one of the most striking of all the *Popule meus* lyrics is headed 'mater ecclesia in persona Christi cantans' (xiv: 72 and note). The neatness and symbolic implications of this would certainly have pleased the man who wrote *The Temple*, and whose *Popule meus* poem also forms part of an allegorized invisible Church.

Liturgically connected, the *O vos omnes qui transitis* and the *Popule meus* (from both which traditions Herbert draws) became joined in lyrics, in Richard Rolle's Meditation on the Passion, in popular treatises like the *Cursor Mundi*. The Latin tag *Quid ultra debui facere tibi* (part of the *Popule meus*) is used as a refrain even in English lyrics (xv: 105, 106),

and variants of this 'what have I done . . . what more could
I do for thee?' turn up even in Christmas carols or in T. S.
Eliot's *Ash Wednesday*. Any one of these strains can carry
with it the weighted, biting oppositions we have noticed—
and many as yet unnoticed: A love-drink I asked of thee,
esil and gall thou gavest me (in a Charter of Christ
poem); for the sins of thy head mine wore a crown of
thorns, for thy hearing of vain tales, I silently took rebuke,
for man's misfooting my feet were through-pierced (Lydgate's Second Nightingale Poem, sts. 26 ff.); where I give
peace, thou makest *debate*, I do thee *weal*, why dost me *woe*?
(in a fifteenth-century short poem). It is not extraordinary
that Herbert's poem in the same tradition should happen
upon a similar wording, 'My *wo*, mans *weal*: and now I
bow my head' (250), but the universal occurrence of these
brief and biting contrasts does make us look doubtfully
upon Empson's interpretation of Herbert's *weal* as a witti-
cism suggesting both prosperity and pustule, and implying
like the bowed head a rather spiteful irony in the speaker.[11]
There are solid reasons why the tone remains markedly
consistent in literary manifestations of the tradition. But
various motifs within it reappear in all sorts of forms and
places, from woodcuts and sermon manuals to two Mono-

---

[11] The Scriptural *bowed head* is frequently emphasized in related poems, being
part of a series ascribed to St. Bernard: opened arms to embrace, bowed head to
kiss, hands to give, &c. There is much emphasis upon retribution in Herbert's
poem, but Christ is not shown as humanly small and spiteful (e.g. Empson's
bowing the head to 'bide his time'); the retribution *is part of* the 'grief', and the
tone is consistently magnanimous like that of other poems using these conventions, which frequently end as I read Herbert's ending—with the notion 'all
is finished—and well finished, if man will but return this love'. These differences offer three cases of the fact that when we give up an ambiguity made
unlikely by knowledge of the whole tradition we give up no philosophical
depth or subtle perception of paradox, but merely a psychological refinement
implying a kind of smartness in the speaker. References in this paragraph are
to Rolle, ed. Horstmann, i. 88; *CM* v. 17111, EETS 66; and for the anonymous
poems EETS 117, p. 649, EETS 124, p. 42.

logues of Christ ascribed to Skelton (see xv: 102–3). An
O vos omnes poem appears as a wall inscription (xv: 108),
and Lydgate uses the convention more than once.

In sum, all the channels I have mentioned serve to keep
the continuity unbroken at least as late as Herbert, and
especially for a man who, as Walton tells us, was so interested in liturgy that he would explain to his parishioners
how certain collects, responsories, canticles, and lections
had come to occupy their places. He could not have got
far in his explanation without familiarity with the Sarum
Missal and Breviary, as anyone knows who has looked into
the history of the Anglican prayer-book. Nor should we
forget Herbert's close connexions with the Ferrars of Little
Gidding. The Psalter rather than the Canonical Hours
was evidently the mainstay of the 'Hours' maintained by
their community; but even so the remembrance of two
other famous poets interested in Little Gidding—Crashaw
and T. S. Eliot—will suggest to us that such a connexion
is not impertinent when we are considering Herbert's liturgical and 'Catholic' preoccupations, and the full weight of
some of his traditional images.

It should be obvious from all this that the notion of a
monologue spoken by Christ, the notion of what such
a monologue should contain, the symbolically used Old
Testament refrain, the special mingling of contradictory
emotions in the speaker, and the general poetic tone of the
whole, were traditional for many generations before Herbert used them. If he created this amalgam anew without
knowledge of the tradition, that coincidence would certainly be most extraordinary; to me it is beyond belief. More
striking but perhaps less important are the numerous relations between the traditional materials and the specific
ironies or choices of detail found in the Herbert poem. A
simpler point of general dependence may be mentioned first.

Structurally, the poem first narrates the main events preceding Christ's condemnation; this set of choices from the
four Gospel Passions follows roughly the structure indicated in the responsories for matins of Maundy Thursday.
These were used, according to the Sarum Missal (i. 245 ff.),
in that striking service known as The Maundy; with those
of Good Friday and Holy Saturday, they furnished motet
texts or were given special musical settings, and may be
conveniently read e.g. in the complete edition of Palestrina,
vol. 32.[12] Herbert keeps to this structure, using details and
phrasings which echo one portion or another of the liturgy
for Holy Week, through about a third of his poem. From
about line 105 the strictly narrative structure yields to one
in which stanzas of reflection or interpretation are felt to be
proper; the underlying metaphor is that of Christ as High
Priest as well as Sacrifice. At the 'now I am deliver'd unto
death' (v. 145) the emphasis shifts to Christ as the crucified
God-King, and with the entrance of the second quoting of
O vos omnes the poem leaves behind both narrative and
meditation structure and becomes a typical *Popule meus*
'Complaint', depending more nearly on the actual *Improperia* of Good Friday. This portion of the poem has a
dramatic 'time', and is said as from the Cross.

But the secret of the power of this poem does not lie in
its initial structural plan, though Herbert was fond of
writing poems of which this could be said ('Peace', 'The

---

[12] The order is not precisely the same in different ecclesiastical 'uses', but we
find that Herbert too chooses to emphasize 'The Princes of my people make a
head' (*Seniores populi consilium fecerunt*), Judas the purse-keeper and bargainer
(*Judas mercator pessimus*), the 'I cannot gain   One houre of watching' (*Una
hora non potuistis vigilare*), 'arise, arise' (*Surgite . . .*); 'With clubs and staves . . . as a
thief' (*Tanquam ad latronem*), 'All my Disciples flie' (*Omnes amici mei dereli-
querunt me*), and so on. Phrasings being largely scriptural, Herbert's independence of tradition here would be conceivable; in that case the marked absence
of scriptural materials *not* liturgically marked out for emphasis would call for
explanation.

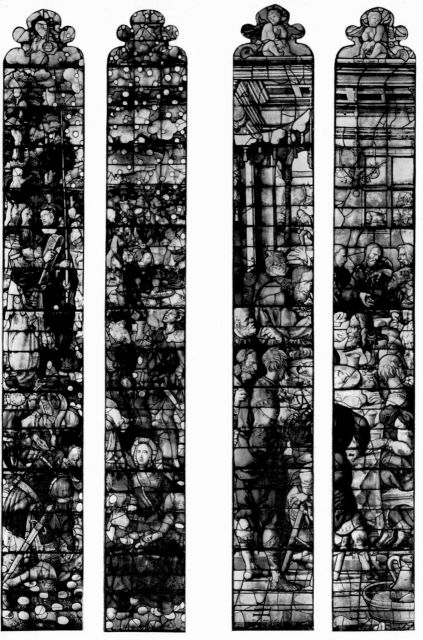

IV. King's College Chapel, Cambridge, window IX north: Manna, Last Supper

V b. *Horae*, 1497 (Kerver): Red Sea, Baptism, Grapes

V a. *Horae*, 1497 (Kerver): Lamentation of Jeremiah; Christ, Isaiah

Pulley'). It lies rather in the density of the serried layers of suggested concepts and emotions, in the frequently almost shocking juxtaposition of these emotions, and in the result-ing variety and constant movement of the tone, from pitying to condemnatory, from tender to intellectually incisive, from brash to gravely meditative, from the accents of the quiet sufferer of other's actions to those of the omnipotent ruler of the universe. These qualities result from the fact that the poem is built upon various types of contrasts, most of them ironic in nature. The most obvious of these types is the series of contrasts between man's actions towards God and God's actions towards man; but the most important type is the related but profounder irony of man's wild mis-reading of the relation between the Creator and the creature, a relation unseen by the arrogant doers of the actions but seen by their Sufferer in all its implications, whence his terrible grief in all its 'mysteriousnesse'.

Subsidiary uses of irony weave their way in and through these; Herbert sometimes merely marks the cruelly neat dis-proportion between what each event or action 'is' to its participators, and what it in truth *is*, the awful, heart-rending joker hid in these unrealized actions of blind men. They do not know what anything they do really is. Men go usually with a pitiful reluctance to their undoing, but these run—to apprehend Him; 'Alas! what *haste* they make to *be undone!*' (34). Or, 'they *seek* me, as a thief, Who am *the Way* and *Truth*, the true relief' (37). 'How can we know the way?' says Thomas, in the Gospel read during the par-taking of the loving-cup, in the Maundy, and Christ answers, 'I am *the way, the truth*, and the life'. To be sure, all these things men seek, and must—thieves, relief, the way, truth; the flat irony with which an omniscient eye marks man's pitiful but wilful errors of judgement is all tied up in a neat play of the syntax.

I have illustrated quickly first this rather neat and sharp
type of irony—the disproportions incisively noted, and used
to hammer on the one nail of man's mistaking of the meanings of events—in order to show how the large fundamental
inherited types of paradoxical or ironical contrast filter
down into the smallest units of the composition. There are
other similar filiations into subsidiary types. One is a kind
of reflection, by Christ, upon the ironic elements in the
situation; in such reflections the blindness of men is shown
as so supremely gratuitous that there is more of pain and
pity than of the intellectual compression noted in the preceding paragraph. Such a one is v. 58: '. . . 'Gainst him,
who seeks not life, but is *the meek   And readie* Paschal
Lambe of this great week.' The contrasted febrile activity
of the surrounding verses—so grievously unnecessary—is
but the other pole of tension in an ironic situation equally
deliberately brought out in the 'dumb as a sheep before her
shearers' passage which Herbert had to read out each Good
Friday Matins (Isa. liii. 7[13]). Or in the *ego quasi agnus man-
suetus* of Jer. xi. 19 (Holy Monday Matins, Sarum Brev.),
or in the *Eram quasi agnus innocens*, motet for Maundy Thursday and familiar through beautiful polyphonic settings. As
in the services, this willingness of the sacrificed one is repeatedly stressed by Herbert: 'God holds his peace at man, and
man cries out' (187; again from Isa. liii. 7, with a phrase
from its fulfilment in Mark xiv. 61, Holy Monday Gospel).

[13] Taken over from Sarum Missal, Holy Wed. A careful reader will wish to
know that I have throughout guarded against 'fake' parallels not really encountered by Herbert and his readers. See the Note on conventions of quoting,
at the end of this book, for exact distinctions maintained in references to Anglican
or to earlier liturgy (clear, I believe, from names used, hence I seldom refer by
title to the Book of Common Prayer). I think Herbert used earlier English
service books, as did others, for private devotions, and certainly for history of
liturgy. The occurrence of readings, Psalms chanted, &c., has been checked by
calendars and service books contemporary with Herbert. Anglican liturgy, of
course, he used for years as deacon and priest, and we know from Walton that
he kept even private offices diligently.

Or, as another reflection embodied in two images, there is Christ's sad summary: 'But *hony* is their *gall*, *brightnesse* their *night*,' 111. To catch the symbolic condensation of this we must be aware that Christ is traditionally honey and the honey-like manna. The last commonplace became especially familiar through the iconographical convention paralleling the Eucharist with the falling round disks of manna; I reproduce this parallel in an example which we can be entirely certain Herbert himself saw—one of the magnificent and beautiful windows of King's College, Cambridge (see Plate IV; also X *b*, XIV, XV). Manna tasted like honey of course (Exod. xvi. 31, read Easter Mon., BCP). Christ is called honey in hymns (e.g. *Jesu auctor clementiae*); even in Prudentius, Moses' rod which is the wood of the Cross turns Marah's bitter gall to Attic honey (*Cathem.* v. 93). The play upon all these traditional meanings makes Donne's inversion in 'Twicknam garden' twice as witty:

> But O, selfe traytor, I do bring
> The spider *love, which transubstantiates* all,
> And can convert *Manna to gall*,
> And that this place may thoroughly be thought
> True Paradise, I have the serpent brought.

Christ was the Brazen Serpent, too, raised up in that place Calvary which Donne elsewhere says was the same spot as Paradise. The context in Herbert is Eucharistic. His Christ as *brightnesse*, the light-bringer, is a liturgical commonplace. The pillar of light, which figures so dramatically in the Paschal Candle service of Holy Saturday, was but 'a cloud and darkness' to the Egyptians (Exod. xiv. 20) while it gave light *to the Chosen People*; the very choice of this lesson from Exodus for Easter evensong amounts to an ironic accusation of those later Jews who, crucifying Christ, had become very Egyptians for blindness. Symbols are used not to write history, however, but poetry; the *Tenebrae* of Holy Week still figure forth the *Egyptian darkness*, in the explana‑ tions of sermons and manuals, and both Exile and Cruci‑ fixion are continually re‑enacted in the hearts of blind men, 'brightnesse their night'. The series of Exodus lessons from Passion Sunday through Easter, in the Anglican prayer book, is a choice depending from the Sarum Use, and it emphasizes and re‑emphasizes conceptions of salvation, atonement, guilt, redemption, which are too ancient and too complicated to be stated otherwise than through sym‑ bols.

In the passages discussed in the last paragraphs—ex‑ amples of comments by Christ in which the gratuitous rashness of man's blind pride is stressed—the tone is one of pain mingled with pity, but a pity too clear‑seeing to be soft. This differs markedly from the tone of sharpness, all but derisory, which marks another subsidiary type of con‑ trast: those in which Christ comments in one breath upon his unused powers, as God, and upon the indignities he accepts. Sometimes the juxtaposition has an exact scriptural or liturgical spring, sometimes not. For example, 'Whom devils flie, thus is he toss'd of men' (191), has a sharpness in the ambiguous antithesis *devils*: *men* which I do not find in the harrowing‑of‑hell passages frequent in the liturgy of the season. On the other hand, 'they deride me, they abuse me all: Yet for twelve heav'nly legions I could call', 155, comes straight from the Palm Sunday Gospel (Matt. xxvi. 53). This quietly makes the deriders ridiculous. The same composed but sardonic assertion of the fact of unused power has the same effect upon the tone in the passage about razing, and raising, the Temple in three days: 'Why, he that built the world *can do much more*', 67. Christ has these jests to Himself, in Herbert's poem, but the bitter

smile which lurks under most irony hovers across even
those hymns and lyrics where some spectator instead makes
the contrast—Mary, for instance, in a fifteenth-century lyric
(xv: 97):

> I know well thu made bothe man and beste,
> Heuyn & erthe & mekyll mare;
> *But now thu lernyst another lare.* . . .

A similar tone accompanies another irony of this type, in
this case dramatic irony proper, commented on in an
understatement: '*It is not fit he live a day,* they crie,   Who
cannot live lesse then eternally' (98). He declines the show
of power which would make fools of his accusers. For this
specific juxtaposition based on 'I *am* the Life' I have
noticed no suggestion in the traditional materials; it is one
of the amazingly few—perhaps three or four in the whole
heaped series of ironic contrasts—of which this can be said.

On the other hand, a more striking 'radical' image in
ll. 129–30 is probably conventional.

> They buffet him, and box him as they list,
> Who grasps the earth and heaven *with his fist.* . . .

The remarks one might otherwise be tempted to make
about 'Metaphysical' audacity and contempt of 'poetic diction' in connexion with the *fist* image lose their cogency
when one notices the *pugillo* in a similar contrast in one of
the most popular of Latin hymns, or when one finds in
Venantius Fortunatus's very famous *Salve festa dies*: 'Indi-
gnum est cuius clauduntur cuncta pugillo . . .'. In the
latter, the contrast lies in the fact that He in whose fist all
things are encompassed should be laid into the tomb; this
poem provided, of course, the well-known processional for
Easter Day. In the hymn referred to, *Quem terra pontus
aethera*, Christ is He who 'holdith the world in his fist';
I quote the phrasing of the widely owned and read *Primer*,

or *Horae*, where this is the ordinary Matins hymn (EETS 105, p. 2; see STC for all but innumerable printings). In this hymn the contrast is not that of Holy Week—the All-Powerful crucified—but the related and traditionally connected contrast of the Incarnation: the All-Powerful become a weak infant, 'Cujus supernus artifex   *mundum pugillo continens,*   Ventris sub arca clausus est'. Both of these poems were much reprinted in the Renaissance, for example in anthologies of Latin poetry like the Protestant Fabricius's. However Herbert's phrasing may strike us, that he himself should have felt it audacious or untraditional is most unlikely; it is even almost unbelievable that he was unfamiliar with the conventional locution in these very Latin poems. Of course, the similar but less pointed antithesis in the utterance of Herbert's Christ, 'I him [Herod] obey, who all things else command', 83, is ubiquitous in the liturgy of the season and in the poetry which sprang from or resembles it.

It is convenient to mention here another radical image which I am sure many readers have felt to be typically Metaphysical in its audacity, wit, and near-indecorum, coming as it does just at the moment of Christ's death:

> Nay, after death their spite shall further go;
> For they will pierce my side, I full well know;
> That *as sinne came, so Sacraments* might flow:
>   Was ever grief like mine?   (248)

This reference to Eve is an undoubted example of dependence upon medieval symbolism, in this case familiarized rather through commentaries and iconography than through liturgy. The *Biblia Pauperum* and the very many illustrated *Horae* (and the Protestant 'Queen Elizabeth's Prayerbook' that copied these) had made completely familiar, to the eye, the parallel Herbert here uses: between the creation of Eve

from the rib out of the sleeping Adam's side and the flow-
ing of the sacraments of the Church from the pierced side
of the dying Christ. '. . . De cujus latere pro nobis fluxere
sacramenta . . .', reads one *Biblia Pauperum* inscription beside the paralleled pictures; 'O vos omnes . . .', &c., reads
another. The third picture is Moses striking the rock. (See
Plates II, III *a*, *b*, XIII *b*.) Herbert's parallel is familiar in
commentaries: in Augustine's Tractate ix on John, or in
Hugo of Sancto Charo's glossed Bible;[14] it was a famous
allegory of the birth of Ecclesia, and so appears, for
example, in Augustine, in Chrysostom, in the Sequence
for the feast of the Dedication of a Church (Sarum M.).
In short, this is a very typical and familiar medieval
allegory-paradox, and when Herbert uses it in the usual
context as cited above, its influence upon the tone is
simply another demonstration of how like 'Metaphysical
wit' is to medieval habits of mind.

In fact, all the types of ironic contrast, upon which Herbert's poem is constructed and which work down into its
details to give it that ambiguity, density, and ambivalence
of tone that we think of as so especially 'Metaphysical', are
explicit in the tradition; the profound and ancient meanings awakened by his use of a very old method are implicit
in the deliberate juxtapositions of concepts and of images,
in the liturgy of what Herbert himself calls in his poem
'this great week' (59). His own words show his consciousness that he is writing a Holy Week poem; that we are less
conscious of its alinements with ritual and with other poetry

---

[14] On this depended the *Bible moralisée*, whose illuminations make the usual
parallel and equate *somnus Adam* with *mors Christi* as usual—with Eve's creation
paralleling that of the Church (a crowned woman with a chalice) at the
Crucifixion; see Plate III *b*, and A. de Laborde's edition. Cf. two sequences of
Adam of St. Victor's (Wrangham's translation, *s.v.* Dedic. of Church). The
threefold parallel occurs among other conventions in the 13th-cent. handbook
for the use of artists, designers of stained glass, &c., the 'Pictor in carmine' (see
below Part II, n. 7; just now available in *Archaeol.* xliv (1951), 141–66).

of the same category results rather from our ignorance than from any lack of care on his part to use those alinements in order to make his poem richer, more suggestive, and more clear. Herbert's originality, like that of much Meta׳ physical wit, is both deeper and subtler than the novelty or the audacity we have been so concerned to remark.

Now that we have cleared the ground by noticing how the inherited paradoxes can filter down into small details of the poem, we may consider the much more complicated functioning of certain large symbolic images embodying these fundamental contrasts. Clearest and most explicit of any of the types of antithesis which are found both in Her׳ bert and in the liturgy are those which directly pose the shocking contrast between man's actions towards God and God's actions towards man. We have encountered some of these already: man stole the fruit, but Christ pays the penalty of a thief's death on the Cross; 'They give me vineger mingled with gall ... yet ... With Manna, Angels food, I fed them all'; Christ planted his vine in Sion, but the crown of thorns he wears is all the grapes it bears; he clave the stony rock when they were dry, while they strike his head, the rock whence the store of blessings issues ever׳ more; each one of his people doth him brave, yet without him each one 'Had to this day been an Egyptian slave'. These came first to our notice because most of them are stated with the same flatness, the same grossly and sham׳ ingly self׳evident absurdity, in the *Improperia.* But more than that, each such contrast is thematically rather than singly used in Herbert's poem—just as in the liturgy of Holy Week. In both, the robbery motive, the vine conceit, the rock gushing forth saving water, the Red Sea of the twofold salvation, as well as other conceits I have not yet mentioned, appear and reappear as do musical phrases in a composition.

The 'thief' motive, emphasized in the Passion story as a result of who knows what dark and subterranean con‑ nexion in primitive religion, appears first in the 'as a thief' of the Betrayal scene (Herbert, 37; Palm Sunday Gospel, Matt. xxvi. 55, and responsories noticed above). Soon thereafter Herbert's Christ says,

> Then they accuse me of great blasphemie,
> That I did thrust into the Deitie,
> Who *never thought that any robberie*:

Christ '*thought it not robbery* to be *equal with God*', says the Palm Sunday Epistle, Phil. ii. 15. 'I *paid* them the things that I *never took*', says Ps. 69, the first Matins Psalm for Maundy Thursday. Herbert's statement of a precisely simi‑ lar concept in '*Man* stole the fruit, but *I* must climbe the tree' (between the two thieves, of course) is related also to another little complex of antitheses between the two trees, as we shall see. Indeed, another echo of the Psalm‑verse used as Christ's utterance, in Guillaume de Deguileville's *Le Pélerinage de l'âme*, exactly anticipates Herbert's connexion; 'I must pay the debt that I never owed', says Christ as the plan is made for Him to descend and be hanged and tacked with sharp nails upon the dry tree which once had been despoiled of 'that other apple'.[15] The Meditations attributed to Anselm also quote these words from the Psalm, speaking of Christ in his Passion. Psalm 69 did not become an Anglican proper psalm for Good Friday until the 1662 BCP, but it is with good reason one of the five 'Psalms of

---

[15] Caxton's translation, folio 63 ff. For the next‑mentioned 'Anselm' Medi‑ tations (ch. x) and their popularity see below, n. 26 and text, and Part II, notes 27, 34. Herbert probably read the long poem—both diffuse and 'Metaphysically' conceited—by John Davies of Hereford, *The Holy Roode*, 1609, to which is pre‑ fixed a commendatory couplet by his brother Lord Herbert. It begins several stanzas with the 'You that pass by. . .' and it uses many of the traditional anti‑ theses, and typological parallels such as Eve's creation: Crucifixion, Moses and the struck Rock, Christ as the grapes pressed on the Cross.

the Passion' in both the 1559 Protestant *Primer* and the 1560 *Orarium*.

This psalm had for long ages provided Holy Week liturgy and music with utterances as from Christ's mouth, including the 'They gave me gall to eat . . . and when I was thirsty . . . vinegar' of the Palm Sunday offertorium beginning *Thy rebuke hath broken my heart.* This offertorium has been made famous even to modern Protestants by the music composed for it, of which perhaps Palestrina's motet crowns all others. Liturgical usage, in giving the words 'Thy *rebuke* . . .' to Christ, anticipates the contradiction which Herbert glances at swiftly in Christ's feeling his Father's *frown* (223). Of course, this unresolved contradiction appears more strikingly, just as in all treatments of the Passion, in Christ's 'O my God, my God! why leav'st thou me', which Herbert emphasizes by one of his infrequent but startling uncompleted lines (215). Paradoxes very frequently spring from the liturgical and homiletic habit of attaching Old Testament phrasings to New Testament events. The Psalmist's 'I paid them the things that I never took' became liturgically Christ's utterance, and the moment it did so there was uncovered, in yet another form and image, that complicated criss-cross paradox which ties together Adam's taking of the apple which brought Death and Christ's paying by 'taking' the death which murdered Death. That Herbert saw this paradox, so fertile in ironies, in just these terms is apparent in his last use of the theft-motive:

> Betwixt two theeves I spend my utmost breath,
> As he that for some robberie suffereth.
> Alas! what have I stollen from you? Death.

The tie or unexpected juxtaposition necessary to most irony—as above in *stollen*—is yet more explicitly given to

Herbert by the liturgy of the season in the case of the vine conceit:

> Then on my head a crown of thorns I wear:
> For these are all the grapes *Sion* doth bear,
> Though I my vine planted and watred there: (163)

The basic element in all irony is an unstated 'real' meaning either in opposition to the ostensible stated meaning or hidden in it by an extreme understatement. The word *grapes*, symbol of fruitfulness, could not carry this ironic weight save for the unexpected twist by which the thorns of the Crucificion are related to the vine Sion. This image is not the Christ-as-the-Vine-on-the-tree-of-the-Cross, Venantius Fortunatus's image in the famous *Crux bene-dicta*,[16] the Vine whence flows the blood-red wine of the Sacrament—although that is an image upon which Herbert fondly plays variations elsewhere in his poetry, as we should remember when we read the 'pierce my side . . . so *Sacraments* might flow' of v. 246. Nor is it the I-am-the-true-vine-ye-are-the-branches of John xv, although it is related to this. Sure of Herbert's familiarity with these images, and knowing his fondness for double and triple significances in his symbols, I prefer to keep these at the bottom of my mind in reading his 'I my vine planted and watred there', in Sion; thus Christ both speaks to and is His People, and the 'grief' of the refrain is more complex.

Similarly, I would allow all three vine images to underlie the stanza just preceding: 'Then with *a scarlet robe* they me aray;   Which shews my *bloud* to be the onely way   And *cordiall* left to repair mans decay.' The image of bloody robe and wine-press traditionally symbolizes the Passion, espe-

[16] Found in many other places, of course, in meditation literature, or, for example in that famous Easter sequence by Adam of St. Victor, *Zyma vetus expurgetur*. On the related image of Christ as the grape-cluster, and the wine-press of the Cross, see Part II.

cially in iconography, and is best illuminated by the passage
from Isa. lxiii. 1 ff., read as the Epistle for Holy Monday:
'Who is this that cometh from Edom? . . . Wherefore art
thou red in thine apparel? I have trodden the winepress
alone . . . their blood shall be sprinkled upon my garments.'[17] The logical base of Herbert's image (based on a
detail in the Gospels of course) is not the mere parallel in
property between *red* robe and *red* blood. Christ's later
scarlet robe (His blood on the Cross), His coat as 'the type
of love', Herbert v. 242, the bloody-robed figure who has
trod the wine-press alone, even the connexions between *love*
and *blood*, all mingle in a single image when a poet is using
symbols and not merely the private creations of his own wit.

But the basis of the image in Herbert's stanza about the
vine is that connexion which makes *Sion* or the house of
Israel *the vine*; though he has planted and watered it, it bears
for grapes only this bitter thorny crown. As Hutchinson
notes, the collocation of thorns, grapes, vine occurs in Isa.
v. 1-7, 'which Herbert evidently had in mind'. So he
surely did, and it had been brought to the minds of uncountable others as well through the services of Holy Week.
The *tractus* for Holy Saturday (Sarum M.), 'My well-
beloved hath a vineyard', is adapted from Isa. v. 1, 2, 7,
and is this image, making the identification between the
house of Israel and the vineyard. I have already quoted

---

[17] For another 'All ye who pass by' poem stating that Christ is this red-robed
one from Edom see Lydgate's Second Nightingale Poem, EETS 80. Herbert
makes important use of this Isaiah image (which is also an anthem for Palm
Sun., Sarum M.) in 'The Agonie'; see Hutchinson's important essay in *17th-
c. Studies Presented to Sir Herbert Grierson*, Oxford (Clarendon), 1938, and see
Part II below. The *avoidance* of careful distinction between 'their blood' and
'my blood' is one of those ambiguities (like the merging of Christ's lament with
Jerusalem's) which reach back into a primitive layer of religious feeling and
symbolism, in the liturgy and Herbert alike. Herbert would be aware too of the
echo in Lam. i (read at Matins, Maundy Thursday and Good Friday, Sarum
Brev.): 'The Lord hath trodden the virgin, the daughter of Judah, as in a wine-
press.'

from the *Improperia* and from various vernacular lyrics that poignant accusation put into the mouth of Christ on Good Friday: 'I planted thee indeed, O my vineyard, with fair fruit, and thou art become very bitter unto me; for thou gavest me to drink in my thirst vinegar. . . .' Similarly, in one of the Matins responsories sung on Good Friday: '*Vinea mea electa, ego te plantavi*: Quomodo conversa es in amaritudinem, ut me crucifigeres et Barabbam dimitteres.' Lyrics, meditations, liturgy, music, had made this symbol from the Old Testament part of the very tradition Herbert is echoing, through hundreds of years of usage.

What is important here is not that Herbert got an image from Isaiah, by way of Christian liturgy. Rather it is that we here see an example, typical of many I could adduce, of what seems to me in truth 'Herbert's method'. We shall also have some light on our problem of what 'originality' is—where nothing is new. Herbert had other kinds of it than that under examination here. But there are kinds of originality which evoke an especially profound response from a reader because they speak to him only of that which he already knows. The power with which Herbert can do this is so especially the thing that matters about his greater images that, as we become more and more the reader who 'already knows', Herbert's dependences show as the most important factor in his originality.

There are several things to notice. In the first place, Herbert's images are not single, appearing once and for all, with determinate limits; they are great themes, stated clearly in the form of an image in some one place, but colouring the phraseology and deepening the meaning of many another passage. This way of using symbolic imagery is precisely similar to the liturgical way of using it; it is a characteristic medieval way, patristic, homiletic, literary. It is partly for this reason that with Herbert as in earlier times an auditor knowledgeable about a whole tradition with its weighted symbols has more chance to be a 'good' auditor— I speak of the *moving* power of poetry, with respect to its richness and with respect to its profundity.

But to be more specific and practical: in the last image treated, by a kind of wrench an Old Testament symbol with all its primitive roots (the blood, the wine-press, God the planter, the destroyer, the sufferer of the destruction) has been made into a vehicle of new meanings through identi-fication with the Christ of the Passion. *This wrench, with its attendant ambiguities and ironies, is made in the liturgy, and was ready made to Herbert's hand.* Such dependence is not un-covered by noting verbal parallels, but by seeing how thoughts have moved. In this particular image, the other prong of the two-pointed irony differs from passage to pas-sage: in the *Improperia* Christ as planter of His people, the vine, reminds them of the vinegar and the gall which have been the bitter wine of their return; in the responsory He reminds them of their choice of Barabbas before him. Her-bert, however, from the vineyard of Sion choked with thorns in Isa. v. 6 makes our minds leap simultaneously to the curse of *thorns* in Genesis and to the thorns of Christ's bloody crown: 'Though I my vine planted and watred . . . *So sits the earths great curse* in Adams fall   *Upon my head*: so I remove it all   *From th'earth unto my brows*, and bear the thrall' (165).

The 'thorns' of all three situations have become the very principle of all mortal imperfection brought on the world of nature by the Fall, all that weary human load which Milton writes of in his allegorical figures of Sin and Death, all those thorns brought upon the *Rosa sine spina* of our lost paradise, without which Love itself does not grow here in the place of our exile, that whole thorny 'world of sinne' whose weight Christ lifts from man in v. 205. This last, minute, logical link between thorns and thorns is the measure of Herbert's 'originality' in this image—and it should perhaps not surprise us that it is just this capacity to see resemblances which Aristotle noted in Poetics xxii as a sign of genius: 'this alone cannot be learned from others'. The basic metaphor, the first great Invention, was found for Herbert; but of such tiny new little movements of the mind as that which his mind has made in using the tradition is genius and poetic greatness made.[18]

When this turns out to be one of the things we mean by calling Herbert an 'original' poet, we could not well praise him more highly. A kind of divinely imaginative logic, this functioning of the mind as it 'sees resemblances' has results for poetry which excite us by their power, not by their newness. What his connexions do is to reawaken into new life whole complexes of meaning, deeper, more ancient and more inclusive than the meanings any single man's experience can provide, and by the same token we cannot follow where he leads with minds too innocent.

The act of supplying through a new connexion another sharply pointed prong for an irony he found ready to his use is something we can observe Herbert doing at several

[18] For that matter, Bishop Bayly made Christ say, in a Divine Colloquy between Soul and Saviour, 'That by wearing thornes, the first fruits of the curse, it might appeare, that it is I who takes away the sin and curse of the world'; of some forty editions of Bayly's *Practise of pietie* between 1613 and Herbert's death he may easily have seen one. It does not affect my point: that Herbert reanimates connexions among elements already carrying weighty meanings, and that hence our response is deepened by knowledge of earlier purports and connexions of images—*if we have evidence for believing that the author was conscious of this weight*. I feel no loss in giving up Empson's Dionysian crown of vine leaves (which would require a temporary lapse, not a movement, of thought, and make nonsense of the double-entendre *thrall*). Still less his 'world, no longer at the centre of man's vision, of Copernican astronomy'. One must furnish *grounds* if one wishes to believe that 'all these references are brought together'. Surely the last is as red as any herring, and we should get over the notion that men had just begun to think of the world as small, or as round, or that whenever they mentioned it they thought with a pang of its position.

points in his poem. '*Now heal thy self, Physician; now come down*', say Christ's tormentors. 'Alas! I did so', Herbert has Christ reply, introducing the Incarnation in his own new way, traditional though it be to recall it here. 'This is the night in which Christ *burst the bonds* of death' (Holy Saturday, Sarum M.) is but one of innumerable similar phrasings in the hymns and sequences of the season. But I have noted Herbert's much neater antithesis at the time of the Betrayal only here and there in a lyric or a hymn: 'I suffer binding, who have loos'd their bands' (47). He quite probably never saw the anticipation of his antithesis in an earlier *Popule meus* poem: 'I bound myself, thee to unbind', or in a Gregorian hymn.[19] The *pattern* of these antitheses in Herbert is, of course, part of the convention— a living tradition, which he in his turn regenerated. The *Speculum humanae salvationis* says: they had great presumption to bind the hands of Him who with His hands created the heaven and the earth; they said 'let Him prophesy', who gave prophets the power to prophesy; they covered the eyes of Him who gave light to them as a pillar of fire. These are in the section on the Mockery and Spitting upon Christ. Herbert's parallel but not identical antithesis contrasts Christ's covered eyes with His opening the eyes of the blind man (133 ff.). Again Herbert's originality consists in sharpening the contrast to a more biting point: Christ is blinded and spat upon, He had with *His* spittle moistened clay and restored sight to the blind.

---

[19] The quotation is from EETS 15, p. 192; see also st. 55. The Passion season Matins hymn *Rex Christe factor omnium*, even though attributed to Gregory and printed, for example, in Fabricius's anthology, would not have had the currency, in England, of materials I present from the Sarum or English Use; addressing Christ, a stanza begins '*Ligatus es ut solveres* Mundi ruentis complices . . .' I avoid here and throughout this essay the claiming of dependence upon specific medieval pieces for Herbert; my point is rather his relationship to an established and diffused tradition. The former would present a far simpler problem for criticism.

Artistic creation is not *ex nihilo*; it is, however, creation, a new life is born. The flame tended, the imperceptible link reforged. We find in the images of the poem various other examples-in-little of what it means to say that newness lies in 'the way' a poet 'uses' a tradition. Since the precise area covered by this well-worn critics' phrase has so often been left as uninvestigated territory in criticism, I will analyse one more example, which happens to have interest for readers of Donne. Although the action of the Kings bring-ing tribute comes in for mention during Holy Week, Herbert makes an original and a brilliantly incisive con-nexion by saying of the dereliction of the disciples (which is liturgically stressed, as all students of motet literature will recall):

> . . . They *leave the starre,*
> That brought the wise men of the East from farre.   (51)

But again, everything is there for him to use save the last small linkage, the supplying of which constitutes his originality.

The juxtaposition of the events of the Nativity and Epi-phany with those of the Passion, of the Word made mani-fest with the Word rejected, is traditional and ubiquitous; the gift of myrrh as symbolizing the death to come is per-haps the most familiar detail. The step was taken early, from Christ-whose-star to Christ-as-the-Star of the adoring Magi, types of the Gentiles who were to worship the incarnate Wisdom of the Father in the Church to come. Matthew's star was connected with Isaiah's 'the Gentiles shall come to thy light, and kings to the brightness of thy rising' (Isa. lx. 3). Balaam with his ass and his '*there shall come a Star* out of Jacob . . .' (Num. xxiv. 17) was uni-versally popular as a prophet of the birth of Christ or Mary, in learned, popular, Latin, vernacular, homiletic, dramatic, liturgical, and devotional literature, and in the arts. In the iconographical sources I have mentioned in this essay, the *Biblia Pauperum, Speculum humanae salvationis*, and illustrated *Hours*, he appears always; the angel and the ass are often the most striking elements in pictures, but the accompanying 'Orietur stella' is equally a commonplace. Erasmus's notes on Prudentius's Epiphany hymns tell us that the star 'indicated' Christ to the Magi, to us it 'represents' Christ. The emphasis upon Christ as the morningstar, the sun, the light, occurring uncountable times in hymns, is too frequent in the liturgy of the Passion season for me to notice its occurrences. I will mention only the long Holy Saturday apostrophes to Christ as 'That Morning Star . . . who knoweth no setting; He who . . . shone serene upon mankind', because they show relation to the very early and very famous Christmas sequence, the *Laetabundus*, in which Christ 'natus est de virgine, sol de stella', a 'sun that knows no setting' born of a star *semper clara.*

Herbert plays constantly upon the theme of Christ as light, and sin, death, fear, rejection as darkness or spiritual blindness. Like the medieval writer who says that the Holy Week office of *Tenebrae* has its name 'in tokening of the dark hearts of the Jews that saw Christ that was the light of all the world and would not believe in Him',[20] so too Herbert conveys both warning and sorrow when he uses this ancient symbol of the Star, whom the disciples themselves left, in the Betrayal scene. The same symbol is used a dozen lines earlier in a conceit that springs naturally from a vivid detail stressed in many accounts; they run to take Christ by night with clubs and staves: 'How *with their lanterns* do they *seek the sunne*!' A translation of the *Patris sapientia* stanza of the popular Hours of the Cross says of

---

[20] This is taken from Belethus's *Rationale*, a text I mention in later connexions, by the author of the *Speculum sacerdotale* (EETS 200, p. 101).

the same event: 'off fals judas be/trayd he was, The maker off all lyghte. Hys discipulis fled a/waye . . .' (see xv: 93). These 'Hours', a widely known set of stanzas, saw frequent reprinting, being incorporated into the *Primer* at the proper 'hours' and appearing in various other places (attached, for example, to the *Speculum hum. salv.*). Although not all translations are so striking as the lyric quoted, the connexion between *sapientia* and *light* or *sun* is a usual one. Another of Erasmus's notes to Prudentius states it in so many words: 'Sol autem Christum designat, qui est sapientia patris.' What Herbert has added is the witty irony of telescoping into one wry observation the vivid physical lantern/light and the old symbol.

Of course Christ as *sol iustitiae*, as *lux et dies*, occurs in so many hymns, versicles, translated lyrics, Christmas carols, &c., that I could not hope to notice them here; Christ is the *O oriens* addressed in the great Oes of Advent, and so on. Obviously it will not do to make too much of the 'Metaphysical' wit of Donne's powerful images of the Son as Sun, especially in the form they take in 'Goodfriday, 1613' or 'Ascension'.[21] That great and famous hymn by Prudentius, *Inventor rutili dux bone luminis* (sung, moreover, at the lighting of the Paschal Candle) plays upon the

---

[21] Everyone knew the *stella splendida* of Rev. xxii. 16, everyone knew the *oriens nomen ejus* of Zech. vi. 12, all but everyone knew Gregory's *Moralia*. A useful note in A. S. Cook's edition of Cynewulf's *Christ* (New York, 1900), pp. 88 ff., gives references; see also 208 ff. on the Complaint of Christ motif. I hope presently in another place to comment not only upon Donne's uses of this convention (see especially his self/composed epitaph, '. . . aspicit eum cujus nomen est Oriens', Grierson edition, ii. 249), but upon other matters connected with Donne's use of liturgy. It seems to me very probable that Vaughan's title for his sacred poems, *Silex scintillans*, has a reminiscence of this famous symbol; Christ is 'silex sive lapis' in the *Biblia Pauperum*, and the *silex*, Christ, in Pru/dentius, is that flint which is the source for our own light, 'nostris igniculis', we are taught thus to seek Light by striking upon a Rock (*Cathem.* v. 5 ff.). There were many editions of Prudentius with commentary; I use the handsome one of 1613 (Weitzio, Hanoviae).

double idea of Christ as Light and Christ as the Rock;
out of the rock's heart, struck by flint, generate new seeds
of light; cf., of course, Herbert's Christ as the struck Rock
(170). Both ideas reach deep into the roots of myth in a way
thoroughly familiar to both medieval and seventeenth-
century Christians. But when Herbert with his star and his
sun image ties together the Dereliction with its opposite the
Epiphany, and simultaneously—using symbols far older
than Christianity—calls to mind all the meanings of the
Deity as *oriens*, a reader trained to receive all these suggestions cannot but feel that strange sense of endlessly pur-
suable true analogies, not tied to the specific myth used,
which it is one of the greatest of metaphor's powers to
awaken.

This property of metaphor to lead us down more paths
than one has perhaps obscured the fact that all the great
images latterly examined can be subsumed under the one
great type of contrast, found also in so many others of
Herbert's poems—shocking disproportion between God's
actions towards man and man's actions towards God. The
contrast is generally expressed, not quite stated, through
some form of irony. Man's blind misreading of the real is
behind all the ironies of this poem, causes that gap between
what in truth is, and how man perceives it, which brings
all these figures under the heading of *ironia*. But to that
special type of contrast just mentioned belong all these
figures of the giver treated as thief, the planter of the vine
crowned with the thorny 'fruit' it produces, the looser of
bonds bound, the physician made sick, the light-giving
star forsaken instead of adored. In all of them we have seen
Herbert take an irony found not by his own *inventio* but
both found and elaborated by those who preceded him; we
have also seen him add some last stroke of genius in the
noting of resemblances which made of a 'tradition' some-

thing new, though it but served to penetrate the more deeply into those ancient paradoxes which lie at the heart of all religions. For the most part this type of ironically noted disproportion between God's actions and man's plays variations upon the great theme of ingratitude—in the tradition generally and in Herbert. The sin of ingratitude, like that of injustice and like that of hybris, has a basic conceptual relation to irony, all being peculiarly failures to read true relations, and involving the substitution of false for true equations. Whether ingratitude be taken in its largest sense (the sense seen in the *Divina Commedia* or in *Paradise Lost*) or in its many smaller daily manifestations, the presentation of it has a natural affinity to the method of irony, and Herbert's frequent use of his refrain to comment with ambiguity upon God's 'grief' at man's ingratitude is a measure of his perception of this natural relationship.

One last large, thematic image using this contrast between God's actions and man's is both more complicated in its relation to primitive conceptions and more involved with the basic idea of the poem than some heretofore examined. In it, man rejects not only Christ as sacrifice, he rejects Christ as high priest, and in that choice rejects the very principle of peace with God and harmony with the divine order of the universe.

Herbert's first poem in the section *The Church* is 'The Altar'; this second he entitles 'The Sacrifice'. On Good Friday, Herbert must read out for the Epistle Heb. x. 1-25, wherein the conception of Christ as sacrifice ('the offering of the body of Jesus Christ once for all') is detailed, and also the conception of Christ as high priest, sprinkling our hearts with blood. And on Holy Wednesday, for the Epistle, he must read Heb. ix. 16-28, with its description of Moses sprinkling the people with the blood of the sacrifice, and again the identification of Christ both with the

sacrificed creatures, 'bearing the sins of many', and with
the high priest cleansing his people (purging by blood,
since 'without shedding of blood is no remission'). It is
scarcely likely therefore that Herbert was unaware of the
suggestions of primitive blood-sacrifice—the healing blood,
the guilty blood, and the rest of it—when he used the
terrible double-edged wish from the Palm Sunday Gospel
(Matt. xxvii. 25):

> Yet still they shout, and crie, and stop their eares,
> Putting *my life among their sinnes and fears,*
> And therefore wish *my bloud on them and theirs*:
>   Was ever grief like mine?

The word *therefore* is not there by chance. That he intended
a double, even a triple meaning here is evident when he
continues:

> See how spite cankers things. These words aright
> Used, and wished, are the whole worlds light . . .   (110)

The third link is, of course, with the blood of the Eucharist,
a mystery always to the forefront in Herbert's mind. The
passage offers but one more example of the attempt to present in symbol that which can be said no other way, in this
case the obscure relations between guilt and the redeemer
from guilt, joined in the person of the sacrifice-priest—
relations and suggestions which Empson labours so hard
and so circuitously to establish. The readers of Herbert's
own day, brought up on this liturgy and skilled in these
symbols, would have caught these and many other and
richer suggestions.[22] Nor would their way into these tradi-

---

[22] One of these richer readings would have been in 'As *Moses* face was vailed,
so is mine,   Lest on their double-dark souls either shine' (138). We make the
single (quite proper) connexion with the blindfolding of the buffeting scene;
a liturgically literate reader caught also the references to the Incarnation and to
the Old and New Dispensation (the veil: Christ's flesh; also, the veil done
away in Christ as high priest; see the same Good Friday Epistle. The symbolism
is explained in 2 Cor. iii).

tional double meanings have been blocked by the obstruc-
tion of a fake George Herbert, a 'cricket in the sunshine'
(Empson, p. 290), a Herbert who never lived but has been
fabricated by a hundred years of reading as if the world
began all over again when Modern English arose.

But there is a further element in Herbert's conception,
and as these others lay ready to his hand in what he had to
read aloud during the 'Great Week' of his poem, so this
too is part of a common heritage, in this case iconographical as well. Immediately following the passages above
examined Herbert's Christ comments ironically upon the
Jews' choice of Barabbas the murderer, therein doing themselves 'a courtesie: For it was their own case who killed
me.' He thereupon concludes:

> And a seditious murderer he was:
> But I the Prince of peace; peace that doth passe
> All understanding, more then heav'n doth glasse:
>   Was ever grief like mine?   (120)

The most familiar element in the image of Christ as high
priest is that which medieval iconography was to ecclesi-
asticize after its fashion—that he is a priest 'after the order
of Melchisedec'; Melchisedec is 'King of *Salem*, which is,
King of peace' (Heb. vii. 2). This typological identification
is repeated in various chapters of Hebrews; some of these
were used as lections for Good Friday Matins, and between
them occur the responsories I have often mentioned, including that 'O vos omnes . . . dolor similis sicut dolor
meus' which is Herbert's refrain. In iconography Melchisedec appears as type of Christ with a *eucharistic* reference,
since he 'brought forth bread and wine' and blessed Abraham, and he appears times without number. Pictured
usually as priest with chalice, he parallels the pictured Last
Supper (and the Manna) in the three popular series I have

mentioned earlier (see Plates X *b*, XIV, XV). Herbert wrote a poem entitled 'Peace' and concerned with the search for it; in it the *Prince of old* who *At Salem dwelt* is this Christ-Melchisedec figure, and peace is in the bread made from that grain which grew out of his grave. The whole symbolism is thus obviously familiar to Herbert.[23] And when we look again at his 'Sacrifice' we see that Christ as the offerer and the essence of the sacrament of love, as the still-rejected envoy of peace, of reconciliation that wipes out the ancient and the forever-repeated breach, is another of the large underlying themes which give con-ceptual reach to his symbols. Christ as Prince of Peace offers and is the very principle of life, love; man chooses rebellion, hate, and death.

The emphasis is in the liturgy too. 'At Salem is his

[23] See also Part II below, pp. 161 ff.; Edgar Wind makes interesting use of the extreme familiarity of this convention in 'Studies in Allegorical Portraiture', *Journal of Warburg and Courtauld Institutes*, i (1937-8), pp. 155-6. Did Herbert see this eucharistic Christ-Peace-Melchisedec figure *in glass*, so puzzlingly mentioned here? He speaks indubitably of stained-glass representations of events in Christ's life in 'The Windows' (p. 67), and he was scarcely the man to notice only the colours, looking at the Melchisedec-and-Last-Supper in the Canter-bury and St. Alban's glass (he need not have gone farther than from Cambridge to Peterborough to see such a wall painting, and he took partly on himself the redecoration of two churches). 'More than heaven doth glass' may be the same distinction as he makes in 'The Elixir', noting how a man may look on glass and 'stay his eye' *or* through it 'the heav'n espie' (p. 184; if historiated glass, there is a double meaning here). My friend Mr. Kenneth Harrison, Fellow of King's College, to whom I owe this last citation as well as all the following references and much aid in connexion with the great typological series forming the windows of King's College Chapel, thinks that the puzzling line from 'The Sacrifice' about heaven surpassing glass is Herbert's comment on the Passion windows in that set. I am inclined to agree, for it is a truly Herbertian remark on the relation of *image* to the *reality* it presents (as Heaven itself to what we see of it through-a-glass-dimly, as 'peace' to our 'understanding' thereof, as the true Heavenly Priest to whatsoever glorious image or type of Him in the glass). Theophilus Woodnoth, Fellow of King's, was cousin to (and intimate with) two of Herbert's closest friends, N. Ferrar and Arthur Woodnoth. Thomas Habington (the poet's father) correctly describes typological glass at Great Malvern Priory (*Survey of Worcs.*, ed. J. Amphlett, Oxford, 1899, ii. 177). We must I am sure think of windows as still *read* at this date.

tabernacle', begins an anthem following the Adoration of
the Cross in which the *Popule meus* is sung. 'In pace factus
est locus ejus', says a Sarum Good Friday responsory. 'I
labored for peace . . . they made ready for battle' is a
Maundy Thursday vespers anthem; it was set, for example,
by Byrd. It occurs in the 1559 Protestant Primer. Herbert's
special uses of peace in this poem, in its connexion with
redemption from guilt, as well as the paradox of the peace-
bringer as Judge, are integral parts of his theme. An
appearance earlier in the poem is his symbolical use of the
dove, most strikingly in 'My dove doth back into my
bosome flie,   Because the raging waters still are high' (94).
The appearance of Noah in a Palm Sunday collect reminds
us that Herbert is using another favourite of typology;
Noah (the restorer of peace between God and man) as a
type of Christ is an inherited convention. That Christ can
be simultaneously the Dove, Love incarnate, the olive of
peace, Noah the saviour of the human race in the ark of
the Church, causes no difficulty in allegorical writing.
Four lines earlier Herbert himself, in the first statement of
the dove-image, uses one of these ambiguities with an admirable effect of combined sharpness and pity; Christ, silent,
tries 'If stonie hearts will melt with gentle love.   But
who does hawk at eagles with a dove?' This dove who
must fight with ravening eagles is both Christ and His
rejected Love and Peace. Herbert almost certainly echoes
Prudentius; treating of the victory of love incarnate in
Christ over fierce enemies, Prudentius speaks of the marvellous change of roles through which wild eagles flee
through the clouds before the Dove descending from the
stars ('Thou O Christ, powerful Dove'—before whom
draws back the bloody bird of prey).[24]

[24] The liturgical references in this paragraph may be found in the Sarum
Missal, and the anthems cited are based on Ps. 76. 2, Ps. 120. The Byrd setting

All these figures and suggestions wear clogs when they must be so much discussed, so much explained, as is always the case when we deal with things accepted and understood at a level which is not that of the deliberating individual intellect. It is out of such overlays of symbolic connexions that Herbert consistently writes, and it is perilous to be too sure of 'the meaning' of his poems without some attempt to be the reader he wrote for.

The instrument of irony which brings in overtones of terrible pathos when used to lay bare the nature of ingratitude operates differently when it is used to point to the sin of hybris. It becomes then cruel as a knife, and the overtones are tones of terror. A dominant theme in the whole poem is the sureness of a justice to come; it is not *sotto voce* as Empson reads it, borne in on the possible connotations of ambiguous phrases, but as clear and awful as the *Dies irae*. It is implicit in the most important theme of the whole poem: man's arrogant confusing of creature with Creator; and whenever it is made explicit in some blunt and dreadful exposure of gross folly, the note of retribution sounds through the verses like the trumpet of the last doom. 'Yet since mans scepters are as frail as reeds, And thorny all their crowns, bloudie their weeds; I, who am Truth, *turn into truth their deeds*'—there is no terror like that with which frail man must contemplate a light which shows all his acts to be what in truth they are; no quarter, no hiding-place. When reality finds man out it is matter for irony; but the joke is a final one. The hardness of Herbert's Christ is intended; 'So they in me denie themselves all pitie' (143); it is the operation of justice we are watching, and justice cannot help to a loophole those who utterly mistake the nature of things, for there is no loophole. The laughter of

is in vol. ix of Fellowes's edition, and see Tierce in the Primer. Prudentius's poem is *Cathem.* iii (161 ff.).

the omnipotent one at man's pretence to power is intended too; it is laughable when the creature forgets he is a creature:

> The Princes of my people make a head
> *Against their Maker*: they do wish me dead,
> Who cannot wish, except I give them bread . . .   (5)

Herbert does not in any passage shrink from the paradox obvious in the last line and a half.

These paradoxes and these emphases upon God's justice, His armed might, the terror and inescapableness of His judgement to come, are no secret ambiguous contribution of Herbert's. Most of the actual phrasings which carry them are scriptural, and the emphases are common in liturgical and other writings of the Passion. In fact, if we were here engaged in determining the actual sources in which Herbert knew the traditions and symbols he uses, and which influenced his choice of the emphases to be given them, it would perhaps be easy to make a case for the *Speculum humanae salvationis*. In the Betrayal section the *Speculum* introduces the O *vos omnes . . . was ever grief like mine* as the climax of a long and damning series of the powers the meek Christ might, but does not, use; it is quoted as a fearful reminder that the Christ who was so 'tender' in the sufferings of the Passion is He who must one day be fell and harsh as the Mighty Judge of all men's various refusals to see the meaning of those griefs. 'He bears himself softly in this world, comes and goes without arms'; forasmuch as He is most tender and most soft, so much the more grievous and bitter was His Passion; and for this does He cry to all those who 'pass and repass on the ways and roads of the earth, that they should bethink them whether ever they saw sorrow, like unto his sorrow'.

Herbert's phrasings of these ambiguities and combined pities and terrors are not usually self-invented. As in the last-quoted stanza, for example, the 'Princes of my people make a head against their Maker', they are full of echoes, and since many of these texts were set to music I speak of echoes in no mere figurative sense. 'The kings of the earth stand up, and the rulers take counsel together: against the Lord, and against his Anointed' is from the Anglican proper psalm for Easter (Ps. 2; *principes*); earlier, it was recurrently used as a Holy Week antiphon. Holy Monday and Holy Tuesday lessons, and in some uses the Maundy Thursday responsories, use certain powerful dramatic verses with a similar *consilium fecerunt adversum me* section, adapted from Jer. xi. 18–20. Set to music as the motet *Eram quasi agnus* (e.g. by Vittoria) this retains a curious Vulgate reading which may explain Herbert's use of the somewhat slack image 'Who cannot wish, except I give them *bread*'.[25] Herbert's Christ says with double irony (two meanings are expressed, neither ostensibly stated): 'They *use that power* against me, which I *gave*' (11); in the Good Friday Gospel Christ replies to Pilate's laughable assertions of his 'power': 'Thou couldest *have no power* at all against me, except it were *given* thee from above' (John xix. 11). Or, echoing Ps. 144,

> *Herod* and all his bands do set me light,
> Who *teach all hands to warre, fingers to fight*,
> And onely am the Lord of Hosts and might . . .   (77)

'Herod with his men of war *set him at nought*' is the phrasing of the Maundy Thursday Gospel. The Lord as God of battles who leads to war accompanies the prophecy of

---

[25] The Vulgate reads, 'let us destroy *lignum in panem eius* [Hebrew, *the stalk with his bread*; King James, the tree with the fruit] *et eradamus eum* . . .', 'cut him off from the land of the living'. No one who has sung Vittoria's angry, smiting 'Venite, . . . panem ejus, et ERADAMUS eum de terra viventium' can forget that this is a resolve to slay the Living Bread, the 'Vine with his fruits'. There is a reminiscence of Ps. 78. 21 (the manna-angels' food psalm): 'He smote the stony rock indeed, that the water gushed out . . . but can he give bread withal '—of course attached to Christ, smitten Rock and Eucharist.

Christ riding upon an ass, read at Matins, Holy Saturday
(Zech. ix). And 'The Lord is a man of war' (Canticle of
Moses), or the Lord of battle and might doing terrible
justice (Canticle of Habukkuk) sound this note of retribution in the Lauds of Holy Week.

Neatly witty, the contrasts recur, all with the same basis
in man's blindness to the true proportions of things, and
each with the same terribly just ridicule of man's presumption. 'The souldiers also spit upon that face,   Which
Angels did desire to have the grace' (181) is Herbert's
succinct contrast; 'Vultum Dei conspuunt, lumen coeli
gratum', reads the same contrast (and rhyme-word) in the
Hours of the Cross frequently found in the *Primer* widely
used for devotional reading. A meditation on the Passion
often published in the Renaissance as Anselm's or as Bernard's has a striking passage on 'That adorable face, which
the angels long to look upon', that face before which all
the great ones of this world shall prostrate themselves—
'they stained it with spittings'.[26]

Herbert does not make private choices of concretions to
carry his ironies, but chooses symbols (the face of God, the
breath).

> Then they condemne me all with that same breath,
> Which I do give them daily, unto death.
> Thus *Adam* my *first breathing* rendereth: ...   (71)

[26] This is the popular *Stimulus amoris*; see Part II, n. 27. The popularity of both
authors accounts for the frequent reappearances of this poignant detail, in
phrasings unmistakably showing its origin. The *Speculum* (Mockery of Christ)
provides one such: they spit on 'that delitable face' 'to behold which the angels
so desire'. The Protestant humanist G. Fabricius imitates it with other such
shocking contrasts in a series on *Christus conspuctus, Christus percussus, Christus
interrogatus*, &c. (*Poematum sacrorum* ... , Basel, 1567, Bk. iii, pp. 192 ff.);
so does the Hellenist Daniel Heinsius—b. 1580; see n. 9 above. It occurs in
Bulteel's preface to his translation of de Mornay's *Three Meditations*, 1627 (STC
18156a), along with Noah, Moses and his rod, Jacob and his ladder, Isaac with
his wood, as types of Christ, and the gall and vinegar as satisfaction for the
juice sucked out of the apple.

Christ is 'the last Adam', and a *second* breathing creates
out of the natural man the spiritual man ('The first man
Adam was made a living soul; the last Adam was made
a quickening spirit'). But these condemners, pure unregenerate Adam, are making the fatal refusal, and the
penalty is eternal death. The great parallel, including that
between God's two 'breathings', is elaborated in the Easter
Tuesday Evensong lesson, I Cor. xv. 45. It would be a
stupidity in us to think George Herbert unconscious of the
theological and philosophical problem implied in his paradox, that it is with the breath *which I do give them* that they
sin. Other poets before Herbert had brought ambiguity
and paradox into treatments of the Passion, and if this
fifteenthcentury lyric is especially succinct, it is far from
untypical:

> And in thy soul I set free will,
> And now I hang on Calvary hill.

(xv: 105, a *Popule meus* poem with the refrain *Quid ultra debui
facere*; spelling modernized)

In Herbert and in the tradition generally, details which
constitute a recognition of man's hybris carry always these
tones we have noticed, of fierceness, of justice to be done
in wrath, or of the flat, all but contemptuous exposure of
absurdity. The Meditation of pseudoAnselm quoted
above points up another traditional such recognition in
'See how this King of heaven is ridiculed by his own
creatures' (ch. x). Herbert has:

> A king my title is, prefixt on high;
> Yet by my subjects am condemn'd to die
> A servile death. . . .   (235)

Certainly the ironic truth of the title of 'King' awarded to
Christ is made quite apparent in the gospels; we are not

pursuing specific sources but noting the sureness with which Herbert's choices of ironic contrasts are those symbolic ones that had been consistently kept before men's minds. More biting than any example of Herbert's use of a *double entendre* to state a truth beneath an appearance is that oracular 'The Lord hath reigned *from the tree*' which liturgy and legend took from a misreading of Ps. 96. 10.[27] The warning of punishment to come which lies close beneath all these exposures of man's folly is plainest in the Old Testament readings; for example, in the Holy Wednesday Matins lesson, Hos. xiii. 11: 'I gave thee a king in mine anger, and took him away in my wrath' (the chapter, incidentally, whence Donne had his 'Death, thou shalt die': *ero mors tua, O mors*). Once establish the habit of freely reading New Testament meanings back into Old Testament images—and multiple significance, deep reach into primitive levels of meaning, follow quite naturally. Liturgy, iconography, and homily had firmly established this as habitual even in ordinary lay thinking. That Herbert had this habit is obvious in the whole corpus of his poetry.

I would re-emphasize here the fact that this array of echoes, parallels, predecessors, even sources, in no way contradicts the statement that Herbert's poetry is highly original. Neither here nor elsewhere in these two essays do I consider that I have weakened its claim to that adjective. To see it in relation to the tradition out of which it sprang is only to perceive with greater pleasure those leaps and those masterful ordering actions of the single human mind by which new relationships are made and new unities created. We have examined the logic of some of these relationships, attempting to define that especial element in

[27] Friday after Easter, gradual; liturgically popularized, quoted in Venantius Fortunatus's famous hymn *Vexilla regis*, it became a riddle-prophecy in the rood-tree legends—see, for example, *Cursor Mundi*, 8486.

'originality' with more precision, and time and again we must see as Aristotle did that the genius for an insight into relationships has in it something of the quality of miracle. But there is no end to the number of factors which enter into a true poet's creation of new from old, and we have only to read any single whole poem of Herbert's to realize it. Were every element in some of Herbert's images as worn and familiar as a proverb, the cadences and rhythms of his language would yet give them for us the uniqueness of something never before heard—and in this judgement we would not be deceived, but merely extremely precise. Tone of voice is a component of meaning. The intermarriage of word with word can be inexhaustibly fecund; scarcely one of Herbert's ancient images but shows it, and only an original poet has this power to marry just those words which will generate new energies out of their intercourse with each other. To re-read 'The Sacrifice', entire, and respond to the living poetic energy which invests it, the chief result as Herbert shapes its ancient elements to his own new and unified form—this is certainly to see that which never existed before born out of that which was. Such a poem is quite as 'original' as we need demand; I should prefer to call what happens 'creation', or use Sidney's old term of *maker*. There is no harm in calling a newborn human child fresh and original, but it does not quite cover the matter. The truest 'originality' in poetry is this miracle of new life. That Herbert has it is only the better seen when we perceive that his originality almost never depends on novelty; *wherein* he has it and precisely how it shows itself is a matter for separate examination with every separate poem. It is quite examinable, and to apprehend this energy that stirs all the old depths into motion gives a deeper aesthetic pleasure by far than we take in noticing what is boldly 'different' and novel.

I come now to the last image I shall examine. It is one already touched upon, but one which is climactic in Herbert's design and which forms the climax in Empson's critique of the poem:

> O all ye who passe by, behold and see;
> Man stole the fruit, but I must climbe the tree;
> The tree of life to all, but onely me:
> > Was ever grief like mine?
>
> Lo, here I hang, charg'd with a
> > world of sinne . . .

It is profitable first to recognize the extent to which 'Herbert's method' (typified by this stanza) is a convention in treatments of the Crucifixion—this method of poignant but wittily sharp antithesis, of act set against act in the neat ironic balance of phrase with phrase. In one of the most popular, most translated, and most reprinted of devotional books, the Meditations ascribed to Augustine, a page and more is given (ch. 7) to a series of powerful contrasts of which these are typical:

I am delighted in eating, and thou art tormented on the tree of thy Passion. I abound with pleasures, and thou art pierced with nails. I taste the sweetness of the apple, and thou the bitterness of the gall. My mother Eve doth laugh with me and thy mother the Virgin doth lament with thee.

Translations differ somewhat, but in all versions the unrelieved beating of phrase upon phrase carries the same tone: the servant doth amiss, the master maketh amends; the tree allured me unto unlawful concupiscence, but perfect love led thee unto the cross; I tasted presumptuously the forbidden fruit, thou sufferdst torments. One has but to glance at the *Short Title Catalogue* to see how familiar this motif, which is simply Herbert's expressed in reverse, must have been to men of Herbert's time. These materials had extreme popularity, were protestantized, recatholic⁄ized, appeared in one dress after another (1581, 1591, 1600, 1604, 1621, 1624, &c.).[28] Part of the set of contrasts found its way into the liturgy; the sequence *Coenam cum discipulis* incorporates a little flock of them.

Liturgically more common is the contrast using the tree alone as the concretion pointing up the parallel between Adam's act and Christ's: 'By a tree we were enslaved; and by the holy Cross we have been set free: the fruit of a tree beguiled us; the Son of God redeemed us, alleluja.' This was sung as *communio* on the several festivals of the Cross (Invention, Exaltation, Mass of Holy Cross). Since the last⁄named was said in Sarum Use every Friday from Trinity to Advent and at Eastertide (some twenty⁄six and more) it is no wonder that this parallel of tree with tree became firmly embedded as a convention, to be echoed in legend and in poem. 'Through a tree forlorn and brought to ground, through a tree to life brought.' Or, 'Adam bit a bite under a bough, wherefore Thy Son has spread his arms on a tree'.[29] Or, says the well⁄known *Cursor Mundi*, telling the legend of the relation of the trees, '. . . old Adam Through a bite brought all in blame,   An apple bit both man and wife   *That tree was death, this shall be life.*' The

[28] They appear in the *Right Christian treatise* and *Heavenly treasure* versions, and the *Pomander of Prayer* of that great popularizer Thomas Becon; I use here the phrasings of the first two, editions of 1591, 1621 (modernizing spellings). A library like the Folger offers various editions not in STC. There were large numbers of Latin editions. That of 1614 has this chapter of antitheses twice, once as Augustine's and once as Anselm's (p. 12, p. 263). Bishop Bayly in⁄corporates them in his *Practise of pietie* (over forty editions; see n. 18 above), also making the parallel between tree and Tree, as does Ludolph's popular *Vita Christi*, quoting the contrasts as Bernard's. The sequence next mentioned is in Sarum M. (Five Wounds).

[29] These two come from the collection of sermons and sermon materials, the *South Engl. Legendary* (EETS 87, pp. 7 ff.), and from EETS 117, p. 615; I modernize but do not alter the concision and force of the antithesis. For the *Cursor Mundi* use of it, vv. 8499 ff., see EETS 59; the *Golden Legend* passage, Caxton, 1493, is in EETS 46, p. 155.

Speculum humanae salvationis has the same parallel, in the section on the Harrowing of Hell. And if these be thought not popular enough to be common property, the *Golden Legend* surely was so: 'the crosse by whiche we ben saved came of the tree by whiche we were dampned.'

The symbolic importance of this identity I shall deal with later, but meanwhile we must recognize Herbert's *the tree of life to all*, used in this connexion with that other tree, as the veriest commonplace.[30] It appears and reappears liturgically: 'Who hast established the salvation of mankind by *the wood* of the cross, that so whence *death* arose, from thence *life* might arise again, and that he who *by a tree had gained a victory* might *by a tree be also overcome*.' This and the similar others were variously used on the various feasts of the Cross—and although it is my belief that Herbert like other clerics of his sympathies used the Sarum service books for devotional purposes,[31] I wish here merely to make clear that we must think of these parallels and these phrases as part of the very tissue of men's thinking about the Tree of the Cross. The tradition got early into iconography.[32]

[30] Giles Fletcher too caught it up, and his *Christ's Triumph over Death*, 1610, though not a Complaint of Christ poem, uses the traditional 'fireworks of contradiction' throughout—Spenserian and antiMetaphysical though he has always been considered to be. The relevant stanza has 'A Tree was first the instrument of strife, . . . A Tree is now the instrument of life . . . cursed tree . . . blessed fruit . . . death to him . . . life to us . . . the Physitian dies, to make his patient live' (st. 13, ed. Boas, vol. i). If this essay were especially interested in Herbert's possible specific sources I should quote the play of words about the blind man (sts. 59–61, cf. also 28).

[31] Herbert's friend and encourager Lancelot Andrewes, for example, used the *Horae B. V. Mariae* (his translator thinks the 1511 and? 1537 Rouen editions) and Augustine's and Anselm's Meditations, for his *Preces Privatae* (tr. Brightman, London, 1903).

[32] For iconographical relations (and an example incorporating a 4line contrast of the two trees) see F. Saxl, 'A Spiritual Encyclopaedia of the Later Middle Ages', *Journal of Warburg and Courtauld Institutes*, v (1942), 107 ff. For Christ as the fruit see especially the diagrammatic trees springing from Bonaventura's popular *Lignum vitae*. The swaddled babe in the tree (see below) occurs in sculptures of the choir, cathedral of Toledo. The Deity (a head with nimbus,

An element so far not commented upon, the notion of preordained necessity, is exemplified in the last-quoted type of parallel—'*that so* the foe who triumphed by a tree should, by a tree discomfited, lose his victory'. This makes concrete an idea which is important, typical, and far more likely to be behind Herbert's 'must' (climb the tree) than is some chance fancy that Christ was not so tall as Eve (see Emp-son's discussion). This tie between the enemy's triumph and his discomfiture—by a tree—is no mere medieval pleasure in seeing things neatly paired and arranged. It has in it a reference to a more real necessity, a part of an eternal plan, 'thy makers provysyoun', as the Complaint of Christ in a fifteenth-century *Popule meus* lyric puts it when making this traditional connexion between the fruit of Adam's tree and the tree of the Cross (xv: 106). The connexion of the first tree with that 'tree of life' which Christ must climb as part of a divine necessity, ordered before the beginning of time, is clearer in the well-known hymn by Venantius Fortunatus, the *Pange lingua gloriosi*: 'When he fell on death by tasting   Fruit of the forbidden tree: Then another tree was chosen   Which the world from death should free.   Thus the scheme of our salvation   Was of old in order laid. . . .' That Herbert did not know Ven. For-tunatus as a great Christian Latin poet would be hard to believe,[33] and it is likely that he knew the frequent use of this hymn during Passiontide, notably the occurrence of its middle section, the famous 'Crux fidelis, inter omnes   arbor

---

usually cruciform) is in the tree under which Eve confronts the serpent, in the *Biblia Pauperum* vignette paralleling the Annunciation.

[33] See the Note on accessibility of these materials, at the end of this book. Ben Jonson could have read this in two British Museum books bearing his signature. No special interest in medieval Christianity was needed; poems like this one came out in anthologies, including one edited by the Protestant Fabricius, with commentary on this very passage, and consisting of the *Paeanas Tres* of Prudentius, Sedulius, and V. Fortunatus, on Christ's life and death, 1568.

una nobilis', in the *Improperia* and *Adoratio* of Good Friday. At any rate, Herbert's 'I must climbe the tree' carries something of this same concept of inevitability.

I should think it clear, then, that the use of sharp antitheses ironically paralleling the tree of death with the tree of life is no novelty of a latter-day Metaphysical poet, and that a considerable *naïveté* is required of us as readers if we are to think that Herbert's particular phrasing of the convention 'has an odd humility which makes us see him as the son of the house' (Empson, 294) climbing in the orchard. There is nevertheless a certain witty strangeness in Herbert's lines, a true ambiguity in the refrain just here:

> O *all ye who passe by, behold and see*;
> Man stole the fruit, but I must climbe the tree;
> The tree of life to all, but onely me:
> > Was ever grief like mine?

Unforewarned, we are struck with something of a shock by what seems an element of pictorial clarity; the hint of actual *identification* of the tree of sin with the tree of redemption startles us; and a modern mind tends to fly at once to those symbols of psychological analysis which we think might help to explain the oddity of Herbert's hidden or perhaps unrealized meaning. But we must not on this account think that the same shock, or the same oddity, was felt either by the writer or by his contemporary readers. Or that, consequently, the explanation explains anything except a difficulty which has come up illegally and is not part of the poem unless our ignorances are part of it (a theory which would extend a good many poems beyond all reasonable compass). I think it can be shown that this at first surprising and contradictory antithesis-identification of the two trees is thematically related to Herbert's idea of the Atonement, and had been felt to be so related by

innumerable writers of poems or meditations or other treatments of the Passion for centuries.[34]

The images which carry this parallelism are often more
shocking and more ambiguous than Herbert's. Empson
speaks of Christ climbing the tree 'as if he was putting the
apple back'; although the tradition in a sense carries this
meaning, it would be too loose and careless an image to
suit earlier minds, too incapable of conceptual reverberations (for things are *not* just-as-at-first, from henceforth; the
knowledge of good and evil still plagues men). A more
daring recurrent image, for a profounder but related conception, is the image of Christ *as* the fruit. *Tam nova poma*,
says Venantius Fortunatus' famous *Crux benedicta*. 'Fertili-
tate potens', 'O Tree of sweetness and glory,   Bearing
such new-found fruit midst the green wreaths of thy
boughs'; 'cuius odore novo defuncta cadavera surgunt';
'. . . Fast in thy arms is enfolded the Vine; from whom in
its fulness,   Floweth the blood-red juice, Wine that gives
life to the soul'. The image was not uncommon or recherché.[35]

If we could examine here the implications this symbol

[34] Empson sees that a medieval tradition in which the Cross was made of the
wood of the forbidden tree makes the 'joke' 'more pointed, and so less odd',
but he does not use what this tradition *meant*, to read the poem with.

[35] Even a carol can begin, 'An earthly tree a heavenly fruit it bare'; Byrd set
it to music (*Songs of sundry natures*, 1589), and I suppose the double meaning is
intended (Nativity, Crucifixion). It happens also to have Christ as '*a Star* above
the stars, *a Sun* of light' (cf. this image treated above). Christ hangs, a ripe
fruit, in Southwell's 'Christ's Return out of Egypt', or see Verstegan's Lullaby
of the B.V.M., or *The Marriage of the Old and New Testament*, by Thos. Middle-
ton (1620; STC 3001): 'The Tree of Good and Evil brought forth an Apple to
cast us all away, and the Tree of Shame bare a fruit to save us all for ever.'
To trace these various points about the tree and the fruit in commentary and
allegorical treatise would be to enter too wide a field, but of course they are
there. For example, the Song of Sol. verse, 'Dixi, ascendam in palmam, ut
apprehendam fructus eius' is discussed as an allegory of Christ ascending
the tree of the Cross; see Honorius's commentary on *Cant. cant.* in the 1618
edition of his works.

came to carry in men's thinking about guilt and atonement, it would be interesting to describe in detail the
lengthy and ingenious use of Christ as the apple, hung
upon the Dry Tree, the same tree on which grew the apple
with which Satan deceived Adam and Eve, and now 're-
established of *that other* apple', in Guillaume de Deguileville's *Pèlerinage de l'âme*. This allegorical romance had
considerable currency; though Lydgate's translation did
not extend to this portion, Caxton translated and published it, and Vérard printed a recension in French prose.
The comparisons between the 'mortal fruit' and the 'bene-
ficent fruit', the invitation to Adam to try 'whether is more
delicious the old fruit or the new', the lady Virginity hid
in the branches, the graft from the Tree of Jesse, the many
references to 'the apple Jesus', the details of attaching with
nails, beating so that the juice flows forth to be a healthful
drink to man, Justice's speech to the despoiled Dry Tree,
that this new apple is hung here 'to that end that *who so
goeth by the way* may see the restitution'—all these are details
which clarify for us the nature of the medieval tradition
that lies behind Herbert's succinct identification.[36]

Like all symbols, this one—while eluding conceptual
statement—is capable of almost infinite variations upon the
given theme, opening up varied but equally 'true' conceptual nuances. The god as the fruit eaten of his people
appears in a use of the conceit in the *Cursor Mundi*, tracing
the tree of the Cross from its origin in the Garden: 'and in
his time suche frute sal give   that alle his frendis thar-fore

---

[36] Caxton's *Pylgremage of the sowle*, 1483, folio 58 ff. It is not uninteresting
that the same text traces the life of Christ as the Sun through a kind of heavenly
zodiac, with the Annunciation in the sign Virgo, Herod's attempt on His life
in Taurus, causing an eclipse, the Baptism in Aquarius, the Harrowing of
Hell in Leo (prefigured, as is usual in iconography, by Samson and the Lion),
and so on. The next two poems quoted after the *Cursor Mundi* may be found
in EETS 117, p. 623, EETS 124, p. 41.

sal live   ne of that frute sulde na man bite   that he ne sulde love . . .' (8491). In one poem the Cross itself utters the same image; 'One fruit for another', it says, a laconic statement of the mystery which all these images are concerned to convey:

> Whon Adam, Godes biddyng brak,
> He bot a bite that made us blak,   (bit a bite)
> Til fruit weore tied on treo with tak; (nail)
> O fruit for another.

In another lyric a different way of phrasing the mysterious connexion between man who sinned, and God-Man who redeemed, shows another characteristic of the operation of symbols; the concrete particular used can undergo a metamorphosis under our very eyes:

> The same mouth that the appyl gnewe, (gnawed)
> In that mouth the holy cross grewe,
> Wheron I dyed for youre gylt;
> Thurgh the herte and thurgh the mylt   (spleen)
> I hadde the poynt, and ye the hylt.

> Ye boten an appyl that thirled my brest. (bit, pierced)

All these poems belong to a mode of writing wherein there is nothing strange whatsoever in a body which is both fruit and vine, in an earthly rood-tree grown out of an apple of Paradise, in an apple which is a sword held in the hand of him who ate it. Symbolical writing (including Herbert's) is confusing only when we read symbol as picture, when we allow the concrete particulars of garden and tree to carry us, by connotation, into alien contexts dependent on our individual fancies. There is an element of the irrevocable in symbols; they have meanings, and limitations of meaning, by virtue of a kind of social compact, and are not ours to do as we like with; it will not serve to read them as if they were images in Keats or Browning or the Sitwells.

Empson is interested to find Christ seeming a child in this metaphor. But indeed there is a medieval image of Christ as a swaddling-clothed babe—*in* the tree whence Adam took the apple, as Seth catches a glimpse of it when he goes to seek for that oil of mercy which he has been told may cure his father Adam of his mortal sickness. This baby is the saving King, and no more connotes smallness or the helpless midnight cry than the healing oil connotes the squeak of rusty hinges or the 'climbing' of the tree a fruit-stealing expedition. Other forms of the legend of the holy rood convey similar relations and meanings in different ways; Seth is given three pips from the apple to place under Adam's tongue, thence they grow into those rods which Moses used and into, finally, the tree which is used for the Crucifixion; Solomon sits under the tree to learn wisdom, and it has a marble stone with gold letters saying that man shall see God Himself reign in this tree, but none understands that this will be Christ upon His Cross; 'that tree was death, this shall be life, and written it is . . . that it came out of that pip that wretched Adam fell from . . . for so began the cross of Jesus Christ'. Seth is told, but does not understand it, that Adam shall not have the oil of mercy for 5,005 years; the prophecy is fulfilled in the Harrowing of Hell, when Christ, having died upon the tree which grew from Adam's grave, cures Adam at last from his mortal wound. 'Man stole the fruit, but I must climbe the tree.'

I have lumped into a paragraph the chief elements in a legend that has similar purport in all its many shapes— for, of course, we have it in Latin, in Old French, in Middle English prose and verse, in preachers' handbooks, or sermon collections seasonally arranged like Mirk's, in the *Golden Legend*, in the Gospel of Nicodemus.[37] I do not think it matters that there is no babe in the Nicodemus version, for example, or that care is not taken to make clear whether there were two trees in paradise or only one. That the 'fruit' whence springs life, love, abundance, freedom from guilt should hang where hung the fruit whence sprang sin and death is a profound statement. That the tree of life is both antithetical to *and* identical with the tree of death is a similar statement. Both are very common.

We need not think of Herbert as knowing these especial images (though how he could have escaped reading Venantius Fortunatus and the *Golden Legend* and the Gospel of Nicodemus I do not see); nor need we even attend to the differences in them; they all spring out of the same understanding. Christ is the fruit, He is the oil of compassion from the tree of life, He is the babe, He is the king reigning from the tree, He is the life which makes it burgeon, He is Sapientia itself, and the tree is the knowledge of good and evil, and when they ate of it they should be as gods—all these are ways of saying the unsayable connexion between the doing of the sin and the undoing of it, and that there is paradox and mystery at the heart of the whole conception Herbert knew and his predecessors knew.

'The Christ becomes guilty' (Empson, 294) is the burden and the mystery not only of image after image through-

---

[37] Convenient partial collections, references, and discussion may be found in EETS 46 and EETS 103, and in the introduction of the latter a list of the sections of the *Cursor Mundi* which deal with the legend; from *CM* comes my quotation (paraphrased) in the preceding paragraph. Various ramifications and useful citations may be found in an article which appeared after this study had gone to the publisher: F. Hartt, '*Lignum vitae in medio Paradisi*: the Stanza d'Eliodoro and the Sistine Ceiling', *Art Bull*. xxxii (1950), 115–45. I owe this reference to my friend Mr. Allan Gilbert. By a convenient chance the same issue contains a *Note* by R. A. Koch (pp. 151–5) providing useful bibliographical data on two illustrated texts that I refer to frequently, especially in Part II—the *Biblia Pauperum* and the *Speculum*.

out this whole poem, but of countless other images and other poems, and in order to catch that meaning we do not need to introduce as in any sense part of 'Herbert's method' the distortions of Paradise as God the *Father's* orchard, of Christ being caught up the tree while stealing the apple for man, from that Father, and hence of *this image* as pointing to the supreme incestuous sin. All these rabbits roll out of one small hat—the fact that Herbert uses the time-honoured 'climb', for the ascent of the Cross, and uses the word 'must', to indicate a far deeper necessity than that which faces a small boy under a big tree. One cannot but suspect that these fancies do not have as their end the *understanding* to which they are alleged to lead, but rather the desire to detect a particular *image* in the poem; that Christ *must* climb in order that we moderns may convict him of the primal incest, and that it is not Herbert's excellence or depth, but his modernity, which we are to be excited at discovering. For it is not meanings (they were already plainly visible) but *the precise images* of modern analysis that we are asked to pursue—even at the cost of thinking that a sensitive poet could write, 'Man stole the fruit, but I must climb and steal it for him', or the equally vapid 'Man stole the fruit, but *I* must *climb* to steal it'.

There are two illegalities here, and both constitute dangers but not inescapable concomitants of a new and otherwise useful method of literary criticism. The first is simple: the reading of a poem is not assisted by intimating that it somehow 'means' all the connoted situations with which chance allows us to endow the author's words. The second is more important and more subtle: whereas it is legitimate to look for and enjoy similarities between the meanings an earlier author opens up, with his instruments, in his myths, and the meanings our new psychological instruments open up for us, it is illegitimate to look willy-nilly for our instruments and for all else they open to us in what he wrote. There is truth at the heart of all myths that men have found powerful; we should be content that psy/chology has taught us to perceive how like each other some of these shapes of truth turn out to be, and not insist that every man who has seen them must somehow, unwittingly, have been taking a look through our spectacles—and that therefore what he wrote somehow 'means' whatever else we can now see through those spectacles had he but had wit enough to know it.

Psychology has also taught us that there are reasons, deep below the conscious level, *why* certain ancient symbols took the shape they took. This is interesting, too, but it is interesting as psychology or sociology; it is not a literary fact. For these reasons are primarily concerned not with the utilizable meaning, but with the earliest psychological spring, of images, and with the sociological uniformities which originally made certain concretions widely usable with symbolic force. Origins are relevant to criticism only if they illuminate meaning and thus deepen feeling (or whatever term we wish to use for aesthetic response). This essay has been concerned to uncover origins (in a restricted sense: *available traditional* meanings), but origins which help to explain what *meanings* there is considerable evidence for thinking a poem actually carried for one of its greatest readers—the author. It is my belief that that should help the rest of us. But that all origins—far back in the unre/corded and conjectural first dawn, origins neither part of a symbol's meaning to the artist nor potent as a functioning such part of it upon us as readers—that all origins are *per se* relevant to criticism it is a pedantry to assume. It is the new form of the old pedantry of substituting inquiry into pro/cess for apprehension of what things are. Perhaps it is the newest form of the less ancient pedantry of biographical study pure and simple; but the biography of elements in a poem, and the study of the history of the mind of the race, must follow the same stern rules as biographical study of authors to be critically relevant.

The meanings a poem carried to its author often lie too deep for formulation without the aid of metaphor; that is why they must be symbolized—but it is not its origins (even when we are sure we know them) that a symbol symbolizes. Meanings are, moreover, inescapably *to* some‐one. We run grave risks when we leave out of count the man who tried to give them artistic form. A work of art is a highly conscious achievement; perhaps the human consciousness is seen functioning at its highest when it tries thus to give form to the formless. The welter has its interest, too, but the excitement of literature is that a mind has shaped into loveliness that which otherwise would lie un‐shaped and dumb. The business of criticism is likewise not with the word unspoken, not with the thing unheard, unshaped, unknown, unmeant, but with the beauty and the power which is taken on by that to which a maker gives form.

I have called these two ways of using psychological data to interpret poems written long before those data were dreamt of 'illegalities' because each of the two has some‐thing other than the poem's meaning, honestly and humbly sought, as object. In addition to the method's undoubted usefulness in explaining those puzzles where earlier authors have seen something of what Freudian psychology sees, before Freud saw it, there is one further help it can give. It can reawaken our sense of the truth in ancient myths and alien images by showing us that we but stare into the same mysteries in our own myths and our own images, so that we may take a living meaning from an old poem. It is because this is not the end result even of some of Empson's applications of this method, careful as he is in comparison with many other users of it, that I quarrel with his re-writing of Herbert. It is one thing to reinterpret the old in ways which let its truth come through to us, to read Christ into the Fourth Eclogue or see Venus as a starry influence, and surely quite another to find a Prometheus and an Oedipus in a poem just for the fun of finding modern intellectual counters. And equally surely it would be hard to find a modern reader who, reading Herbert, suddenly *felt* the true importance and overwhelmingness of the guilt he has been freed from because for the first time he could relate it to something which *does* move him—the sin of incest.

To feel suddenly that Herbert may be important because he has some Freud in him is not the same thing at all. It would be easy to find a reader who is excited by the possible presence of Freudian theories in old poems—and plays. And hard to find one who suddenly saw in the duty laid upon Hamlet what Hamlet says he sees in it, and felt the tragedy of *that* sight, by the route of this new excitement. Easy to find one who is pleased to have the governess from Henry James to add to the list of the-spinsters-with-the-hallucinations; hard to find one who *thus first felt* to its bitter depth the awfulness of evil incarnate, as James un-covers the bared face of it in *The Turn of the Screw*. The same simple test holds in all the cases: if it is the theory we are chiefly excited about, the great thing will be to detect happily the traces of the theory in the work; it will not be the poem, and the poem's own *raison d'être*, which suddenly seem unreplaceably beautiful, and unendurably true—for it is not these which have had our attention. There is thus loss, though there is no great harm, in looking at plays and poems to see whether they know what we know. The harm comes when we become willing to overlook a certain

amount of violence done to the play, done to the concep⁄
tion clearly central for the poet, done to the theme, to the
image—in the interest of finding in a piece the clichés of
our own favoured patterns. Solomon's wisdom was not
directed towards critics, but it is not the true critic either
who is willing to cut the baby in two to have some share
in it himself. The line does not seem at first easy to draw,
for all good reading is concerned to find meanings valid to
ourselves. But there is actually a fairly clear difference be⁄
tween the pleasure of contemplating a poem's meaning and
the excitement of finding our theories in it. The second may
make the images extremely interesting to us, all the more
interesting usually for being extracted and laid upon the
table; only the first makes images moving, *in* the poem
they are in.

The reason why such discoveries (or pursuits, rather) do
not affect our feelings, but rather interest and amuse, is not
far to seek. It lies in the fact I have already noted, that the
history of an image, or even the subconscious psychological
reasons we try to assign for its taking the specific concrete
shape it took, simply are not the meaning of that image. It
has often taken on through centuries of use such layers upon
layers of consciously apprehended significance, which give
richness and moving power to its use in poetry, that we feel
far more loss than gain when its possible primeval meaning,
or its subconscious base, is substituted for these. What this
substitution does is remove the image from the domain of
metaphor; a psychological datum, like an historical one,
may explain and rationalize a metaphor—but a poet is not
trying to show how his metaphors come to be, he is using
them to think with. It is a long time since incest as the
actual, the committed, primal crime has seemed as shock⁄
ing and as urgent to a thinking man as does the total philo⁄
sophical problem involved in the presence of evil in the

world, its cause, and its remedy. When we have thinned down the symbol to its possible first shape, or base, we have straightway to 'translate' that incest-image too, before we can feel it, and feel through it all the implications that are involved; and it is a question whether Herbert's own traditional symbols, unrefurbished, do not come through to us with more power. Provided, of course, that we still have the slightest interest in the subject of the poem. Nothing we can do to this poem can prevent it from being a poem about man seen as guilty of wrongdoing, and faced with the choice of redemption; if we no longer see this as a problem, then presumably we may as well treat the poem as a mine for extracting anthropological and psychological data, and salvage at least that from it.

I must end with something of an apology, and something of a hope. In spite of all the corrections I have wished to make in it, Empson's reading of Herbert's 'Sacrifice' yet reached certain depths of meaning which are not only truly 'in the poem' (in every reasonable sense of those words) but also which were seemingly missed by the many generations of critics who have been content to ignore it. This outright addition to our understanding seemed to me to result from one habitual—and invaluable—manner of proceeding: this critic sank himself into the images as into the pit, tried every conceivable path into their meaning. He has recognized an incontrovertible fact, and I too wish hereby to recognize it: that it is of the nature of metaphors to be infinitely suggestive, and that 'what do they mean' is an inquiry that cannot possibly ever be finished. This has its troublesome side, but it is the basis for poetry's claim to be a mode of knowing truth.

It is because this newly emphasized method of getting at the meaning of poetry is so fundamentally trustworthy a method that I have been at pains to criticize parts of Empson's application of it so rigorously. I have said sharp things of it, and I apologize for the sharpness, which was a rhetori-cal device on my part, but I do not apologize for the things. The usefulness of this new emphasis in criticism, resus-citated after some four or five hundred years and given a new slant, will depend upon whether we deify what we have found, determined to have no other gods but it, or, as we might do, add it—a useful but humanly fallible tool —to the tools we have got from the hands of those who preceded us.

The tools they passed on to us—especially the tool, quite as insufficient used alone, of accurate methods for deter-mining possible meanings in poems to their authors or to their first publics—are precisely those which can show up our new errors, and excesses, and illegitimacies, and pedantries, for what they are. But we shall probably be no less single in our devotion to a new critical religion than our fathers. We shall in our turn tell the images what to mean instead of listening to what they say. We shall quite innocently rejoice in the new cubits we add to the stature of poets whose protagonists must by killing their uncles set right Time itself gone out of joint—and not even notice the narrow thinness to which we have brought the central figures of our new case histories, how they rattle around in plays too large for them, and how the Trees we set them to climb will no longer hold the weight of the world's sorrow, so long and so various and so old before ever we were born to set our special label upon it. The modern pedantry of valuing a poem because it has 'all the Freudian stuff, what fun' (Empson, p. 282), so like the pedantry of 'intellectual climate', or like the one before that, 'author's development', or like any of the ones before those, will seem to us quite honestly the way to enjoy the poem. We shall do a braver thing than all the Worthies did if we escape adding to this another modern critical attitude which will turn mere in-completeness into real arrogance—the attitude that our reading is somehow likeliest to be the truest one, 'better' even than the author knew—not even just 'better for us'. This can be, no doubt.

Perhaps any critical advance is accompanied by this single-mindedness. Perhaps this is the best that can be done, and future generations, though they find us wrong-headed and stubborn, will grant that at any rate we emerged with a few undeniable facts—that knowledge of Freudian symbolism can help to uncover realities in poems written long before Freud, that a poem itself (when we use every help to its reading) supplies the primary data by which any interpretation of it can be checked, that ambiguities and ironic reservations are genuine components of meaning, and the like.

But this essay has been written in the hope that we can do better than this. Other ages have found it possible—some others. It would be a happy thing if the criticism of poetry could escape what seems to be the universal after-math of throwing out 'absolute' standards of value—the setting up of ourselves as the Absolute. A large position to relinquish, but insecure. If we could bring ourselves to this act of self-conquest, it is possible that we should gain back a past. It has seemed to me that great symbols and images, powerful over centuries, have, and have had, meaning at so profound a depth that if we are willing to investigate the meanings they have held for those others we shall be able to see in the images certain still believable significances which our own lives and our own times might never have opened up to us. I have taken this poem and this particular critique as a 'test case', partly to show how various habits and tools of scholarship (tools which the newer criticism would like to relinquish) can serve as a check upon certain newer methods, and can show us when they are carrying us not into but away from the poem.

Yet, of course, no one would devote all these pages to the examination of a single poem's relation to a great tradition who did not believe that this would of itself serve to illu-minate the poem, the poet's other work, and the minds we bring to the reading of many another piece of literature unmentioned here. Even so, it will seem to many too long a road for criticism to set for itself. Too much 'learning'. Too many footnotes required. There is no answer to this. It is a long road. All the same, I do not know why we should not walk in it. Who are we, that our time is too short to understand George Herbert?

PART TWO

GEORGE HERBERT has used in his poems a number of other symbols, drawn from Christian and ecclesiastical tradition, which were familiar to the Middle Ages and the Renaissance and have since become obscured to us. Their very presence sometimes goes unnoticed, and the dimming out of meaning consequent upon this change in the sensibilities of his audience damages some of Herbert's poems appreciably. The waste for us is more unhappy by far than the unfairness to him. The symbols have rich histories and are interesting in themselves, and the poems are sometimes beautiful, sometimes puzzling but attractive, sometimes intense and moving even when imperfectly understood. To explain and illustrate (not by bringing new light but by letting the old shine through again) is not quite all of this essay's purpose. I further wish to discuss these matters as a demonstration of what characterizes writing in the symbolical mode.

Herbert's outlook on life and on poetry is greatly at variance with that which we oftenest encounter in a Western nation in the twentieth century, but not greatly at variance with that which most of the critics of our society (and all modern poets are this) have pointed to as an outlook we sadly need. I do not refer to the fact that Herbert is a Christian poet. In fact my point may be harder to make because all the poems I shall examine are deeply sunk in the matrix of orthodox Christian thinking. I refer to Herbert's unselfconscious exhibition of a way of looking at life and at truth which is at the very heart of the aesthetic experience: he reads the spirit in the letter. Not *into* but *in*; he writes in symbols because he thus sees the world, both outside and inside himself; he sees it as a web of significances not as a collection of phenomena which we may either endow with significance or leave unendowed. He writes

not of events and facts, but of meanings and values, and he
uncovers rather than creates these meanings. He 'reads'
them in the universe, of which he is a humble but unde-
tachable part. Things, experiences, and events convey
values to him just as metaphors convey them—by presenting significances which escape more literal statement. He
not only respects the world of meanings thus presented as
real, but in turn, like all poets, he embodies in metaphor
these values he cannot say otherwise. One result is that what
we take from his poetry is not chiefly his experience, nor
even his meanings for it, but thoughts and feelings which
will carry all the meaning our own lives and selves make
us capable of relating to them. This perception of all things
in their metaphorical dimension is the greatest single dis-
covery we can make concerning the quality of life by reading the poetry of the sixteenth and seventeenth centuries. It
was far from new then; for these centuries it was not a dis-
covery but a habit. It is a mode of approach to truth which
Western culture has slighted for some centuries, with bitter
results.

Not only acceptance of universal meaningfulness but
systematic correspondences between meanings—these are
basic assumptions regarding the nature of reality which
underlie all writing or other arts in the symbolical mode.
Such writing is not different from ordinary figurative
writing in kind but only in degree; all metaphors operate
like symbols, but not all metaphors imply as symbols do
a whole system of traditional and publicly known correspondences. The insight into truth by means of metaphor
marks the 'aesthetic' province and method *par excellence*, is
poetry's *modus vivendi*, but all the great religions have used
it, and in that connexion we meet it when we study 'myth'
—in the rehabilitated modern sense of that word. The history of all modern poetry with any claim to be called great

is the history of our attempt to recapture this way of viewing the world; and it has been the extreme of the method, the symbolical rather than simply the figurative mode, which our poets have embraced. This is partly because our need to regain lost ground has been recognized as so great, our concentration on the rationalistic, on the objective, on the workable as the only form of the valuable, has been seen as so dangerous. Yeats perhaps reached deepest by his constant struggle to maintain this world-view and convey it through this mode, though Eliot comes quickly to mind because he has attempted it in the realm of Christian symbolism as developed in the West, Herbert's own realm. However, the essential characteristic of this way of perceiving and presenting reality—that it sees and shows all things as incarnations of the values which inform them—is confined to no single religion, or poetry.

Nevertheless, although there are many such patterns of symbols, it is necessary to *believe* whatever set belongs to us. One desperate modern substitute for belief—investigating and comparing the various sets of meaningful symbols, and then dressing ourselves up with a set we find 'interesting'— is just another form of the descriptive, critical, rationalistic approach to what is real. It produces anthropology not literature, and is not an aesthetic activity but one motivated by our customary desire to use whatever instrument will effectively get us something we would like to have. All that can remain of a self-deception is the truth of the motive behind it; we cannot get a myth for ourselves by ardently wishing we had one. It may be that future centuries will show the actual poetry we have produced as vitiated by reason of this difference between self-conscious desire and self-forgetful belief.

It is far too soon to tell. Only a bumptious intellectual pride would permit us to state as a fact that, for example,

Eliot's reading of the situation is wrong when he speaks of 'redeeming the time' and 'preserving the Faith alive through the dark ages before us', while the world finishes out its doomed experiment of forming 'a civilized but non-Christian mentality' (the conclusion of 'Thoughts After Lambeth').[1] For there have been eras in which poets have preserved certain kinds of truths until history should allow them to be true again, eras generally of fanatical devotion to some particular shape of truth and in situations where survival itself was at stake. So as in a vial poets and the readers of poetry preserved pagan myth through the centuries during which Christianity struggled for establishment. The usual method of such preservation adds a cubit to what it preserves, for whatever is too true and too valuable to lose simply goes underground as allegory. It does not hide; it just stays true but true in another mode. The gods have never died, the fertility cup is the Grail, Venus is as alive in the great 'continued metaphor' or allegory which she has become in Spenser as she was in any temple where she was worshipped. But these symbols were not a game or an exercise; they were believed; the life of truth in the aesthetic realm depends upon belief. Chaucer's Jove and Saturn were believable and believed symbols for the mysterious but orderly causation of human temperament in the jovial and the melancholy man, the life-principle betokened by the Grail was seriously regarded as divine, the Elizabethans in truth respected Love as creator and preserver of forms. If our poetry dies, and our understanding of the great symbols with it, it will be because we gave them not our belief but only our respectful critical attention.

This failure, if it turns out to be such, will not be a mysterious one. Symbols are unbelievable and hence sterile only in case they are not true symbols, only, that is, in case

---

[1] Eliot, *Selected Essays*, New York (Harcourt Brace), 1932, p. 332.

we are not able to use them to epitomize and figure forth all our own 'new' meanings, and thus to make them repre/ sentative of our completest reading of the true and the valuable. A danger in our own case is that we too much think of the 'symbolic' as opposed to the 'scientific'; more than one of our poets seems to require of us an intermittent shutting of the eye to all those kinds of truth which our world has found most useful and productive. This accom/ paniment of self-deception has not been required of any society which has produced a living myth or a valid set of symbols. Such a one-eyed seer is not that reader of meanings in the universe, that humble part of all he sees, whom I described in speaking earlier of Herbert. The true scientist fits the description better, and with the true ones, who are at the heart of the endeavour, poetry must come to terms. The self-defeating antipathy to 'science' among exponents of a poetic world-view is precisely as dangerous as its parallel, the assumption by arrogant empiricists of the com/ pleteness of their own view of reality. A contradiction rather than a difference has come to be assumed between the rationalistic, objective, empirically verifiable concep/ tions of what life is and the poetic, aesthetic, contemplative conceptions. The erecting of this contradiction is the work of those who are willing to know only the one kind of con/ ceptions or the other. The poet Yeats, to say nothing of many literary critics now writing, is not exempt from this form of pride.

It remains true, however, that our most general inade/ quacy does lie in what our poets and critics have striven to remedy—the gradual stultification of our power to contem/ plate and enjoy meanings. Herein lies the relevance of George Herbert and his way of writing to the predicament we now find ourselves in. We need practice. The modern mind is not a flexible mind outside its own set of pre-suppositions. This is not I dare say confined to the modern mind, but we cannot affect any other. Our own poets have shown us that we need to relearn the very alphabet of symbols, and more than that the habit of mind which accompanies this way of looking at the world of experience. Things have come to such a pass that we do not even recognize great numbers of the symbols in that group which has been most important in the development of our own branch of Western culture, those evolved by medieval and Renaissance art and letters to express Judaic-Christian religious ideas. In this respect our new 'dark ages' have already lasted some little time; we are roughly, say, the mid-sixth century. And instead of saving the inner truth of symbols by allegory, as our predecessors of an earlier Dark Ages did with Cybele and Saturn and Leda, we have for the most part chosen to forget whatever we have not thrown away. Moreover, the combined secularization and declassicalizing of education have gone far to produce a race of readers so literal-minded that they cannot read any poetry of any kind at all. As long as Phoebus Apollo remained alive in metaphor, a Christian poet had more chance of being understood when he wrote about Christ the never-setting Sun. Add to the attrition of myth-in-metaphor the attrition of religion, the greatest and most pervasive of all folk-poetry, and there must follow a grasshopper plague of explainers-of-poems, for the child who has never met mystery in the shape of the inexplicable Trinity or symbols in the Alpha and Omega of the church window becomes the adult who does not know there are any mysteries until he is beaten on the head by the tragedy of his own destiny. The idea that there are no mysteries has not served the twentieth century very well. Seeing no riddle to be read, men cut the whole world into a vast image of the shadow cast by their own selves. Poetry cannot be got whole into that image.

It seems to me important, in addition, and especially when earlier poets like Herbert are in question, that we should not fool ourselves by thinking that we can 'contemplate and enjoy' without a full understanding of the language a man uses. Variants of the idea that we can quite well do so are popular with many currently fashionable critics. It is true that we can never sit within the very mind of the author or the first public of poems three centuries old, yet it is a very good thing for the understanding of poems that we should try. That effort does not constitute the aesthetic experience which poetry exists to give. But no sensible man need confuse learning how to read with reading, and no humble one will be afraid that an interest in the author's intention (especially in its relation to what response he could possibly have been counting on in his readers) must somehow kill one's own authentic reaction. What kills good poems through the eye is a reader's blind determination to see nothing in the round world but himself, and the wish to read without attending to what the author could have had in mind is one form of it. In poetry which uses symbols, uninformed reading amounts to a kind of mumbo-jumbo, and poetry becomes a fetish rather than a mode of insight into the depths of life; modern criticism is indeed not innocent of this fetish-worship. It is necessary to be unurbanely forthright about these matters nowadays, especially in America, for the pressure of anti-intellectualism (scarcely confined indeed to our more outspoken country) has rendered suspect the kind of criticism of early poetry which brings scholarly knowledge as well as critical acumen to bear upon a poem. In fact, writing which uses symbols shows up the whole set of confusions with especial clarity, because symbols are great metaphors with publicly recognized significances, and to deny ourselves the use of every possible help to their understanding—inside the poem, outside it, behind it and before it and alongside it—is simply to prevent the elements of the poem from exercising their full power upon us. These helps to understanding are admittedly instrument, not end. The essay which follows is instrumental. As for the reading of the poems, that read⁄ ing which this essay is designed to assist, every man must do that for himself.

Such instruments can, of course, be more needed or less for different poets or by different readers. Because Herbert writes in what I have called the extreme of the method— the symbolical mode—he needs commentary for many of the same reasons that Yeats and Eliot need it; this last need is one which modern criticism has seen and admirably met, furnishing us with just such instruments to help out our reading as this one. Unlike these poets, Herbert did not need commentary in his own time, because when he wrote in symbols to which he gave his belief he used a language commonly known to him and to most of his readers; he had the good fortune to live when there was a language of images in which a man could understandably say to others the truth that was in him, as much of it as he could see. It is also true that for us now Herbert's case is more deceptive than that of these modern poets, for not only do we still partially know his language but we can read him in a lesser way without knowing it, and without missing the know⁄ ledge. We can read Herbert as history, without much help; that is, we can understand and sympathetically follow him in certain mental experiences he had. But it is very difficult to read him as poetry, filling his metaphors and large under⁄ lying symbols with meaning for our own different world, unless we have found out certain basic and common mean⁄ ings of his images as one finds out the basic and common meanings of unfamiliar words in the dictionary.

Thus the reasons why we need to master the language of

a poet's images lie in the very nature of metaphor's way of working. It is in so far as they are figurative that poems most defeat time, and carry the weight of meanings which illuminate us here and now. Sidney saw very truly when he showed the relationship between poetry's power to out-wit the ever-changing particularity in which universals must always be clothed to man's sight, and her great speak-ing images. It is the true operation of metaphor to allow this filling of the bottles with new wine which yet does not burst them because it was always there. Without this the poem stays locked, an historical curiosity, in the time that gave it birth. But although this is what makes any good poem contemporaneous with the reader, it is paradoxically not very likely to happen until he has freed himself of his own 'here' and his own 'now' and entered into the full pur-port of alien images, like an inhabitant, as to the manner born. Then can he read them, throwing the lie in Plato's teeth, as true 'images'; who does not understand the poet's language can read only the lies the poets told. The language of the symbols used by a seventeenth-century religious poet is not one a modern reader can pick up unthinkingly. (There are some kinds and aspects of poetic language which sympathy, almost unassisted, can teach.) Yet only the images a man understands as he understands his own mother tongue can work upon him after the immemorial fashion of all metaphor. Only thus will they have for him that loveliness which ravishes the understanding, and only thus will he experience what I have called the peculiar func-tioning and contribution of the arts: the insight into a world of values and meanings not otherwise either open to man's sight or conveyable to his fellows.

§1. *Images as Language*

Typical of this problem of figures as a language is a group of Herbert's poems we may look at first. All of them use the set of conceits clustered around the ancient symbol of Christ as the miraculous grape-bunch which figured forth the inheritance of the Chosen People, crossing over Jordan into the Promised Land.

One of the oldest of the Old Testament 'types', this has a history in graphic works of art—glass, illumination, wood-carving, enamels, painting, book-illustration—which shows it as popular from the eleventh or twelfth century until considerably after Herbert's time; and the very situa-tion itself of one of his poems, 'Love-joy' (p. 116),[2] springs from this iconographical use. It is closely connected with various other symbols or conceits: Christ in the wine-press of the Cross, the saving drink of Blood (Wine), Sion or the Virgin as Vine, Christ as the Fruit or as the Vine. These connexions are in Herbert as well, and often explain what seem to be eccentricities, ellipses, or inexplicable leaps of the thought. In fact, a number of the *kinds* of assistance given to a reader by understanding the traditional language of images are illustrated in this little set of poems or refer-ences: such understanding clarifies the very title and basic invention of 'The Bunch of Grapes', making apparent its admirable unity and thematic use of imagery; it renders intelligible an image in 'Divinitie' (p. 134) and deepens the significance of those in 'The Agonie' (p. 37) and 'Good Friday' (p. 38); it makes us more sympathetic readers by taking the over-ingenuity out of 'Love-joy' (p. 116); and it reveals the presence and operation of central impulse (im-pulse rather than concept) which gives the many and

---

[2] F. E. Hutchinson's edition, Oxford (Clarendon Press), 1941, is used throughout; see the Note at the end of this book on conventions of quoting.

VI. *Biblia Pauperum*, block-book, B.Mus.: Red Sea, Baptism, Grapes

VII. *Speculum hum. salv.*, block-book, Bodl.: Cross-carrying, Isaac, Slain son, Grapes

a

b

VIII *a*. Bedford Hours, B.Mus. MS. Addit. 18850, f. 84ʳ, *c*. 1423: Cross-carrying, Grapes

VIII *b*. *Les figures de la Bible* (Vérard): Isaac, Cross-carrying, Widow of Sarepta

IX *a. Speculum hum. salv.*, B.Mus. MS. Harl. 3240, f. 15ᵛ, xiv c.: Bapt., Sea of brass

IX *b. Speculum hum. salv.*, B. Mus. MS. Harl. 2838, f. 14ᵛ, xv c.: Bapt., Sea of brass

various poems of Herbert's book an organic though not a methodical unity.

'The Bunch of Grapes' (p. 128) is most involved with our problem, for it has as one side of its poetic subject a description of the very workings of typology, that is, of the reading of the Old Testament as filled with symbolical types to be fulfilled in the New. 'God's works are wide, and let in future times', says Herbert; 'Their [the Jews'] storie pennes and sets *us* down'. This is no academic notion to him; the poem is a moving record of his state of mind, and it is he, George Herbert, whose approach to Canaan, whose inability to distance himself from 'the Red sea of shame', whose weary rebellious murmuring, are all chronicled before they happened, in the figures and types of the ancient story. With 'Alas! our murmurings come not last', a self-accusation that brings on self-defence, comes one of the characteristic shifts of tone which give living movement to Herbert's poems, and there is almost a pert defiance in 'But where's the cluster? where's the taste　Of mine inheritance?' If he has the Israelites' sorrows, their 'sands and serpents, tents and shrowds', why may he not have 'their joy'? He had thought he captured it once—this is the poem which begins

> Joy, I did lock thee up: but some bad man
> 　　　Hath let thee out again:
> And now, me thinks, I am where I began
> 　　　Sev'n yeares ago:[3]

---

[3] This poem is not in W. (the Williams MS.) and may have been written later, at Bemerton. Herbert decided during 1625 to take orders, was ordained as deacon by July 1626, as priest in Sept. 1630, and died in 1633. But Hutchinson's warnings (in the introduction to his edition) against over-specific autobiographical interpretations of the poems are very greatly needed if we are to save Herbert from the sentimentalizing commentary under which Donne has suffered, and Herbert's difficult and fluctuating progress from 'the Red sea' 'towards Canaan' has rather to do with the universal human struggle for a willing and willed submission.

Herbert's answer to his own defiant 'where's my inheritance?' is as moving, once we grasp the symbolism in
which it is couched, as that other simpler 'Me thoughts I
heard one calling, *Child*!' with which every modern reader
of poetry is familiar.

> But can he want the grape, who hath the wine?
> I have their fruit and more.
> Blessed be God, who prosper'd *Noahs* vine,
> And made it bring forth grapes good store.
> But much more him I must adore,
> Who of the Laws sowre juice sweet wine did make,
> Ev'n God himself being pressed for my sake.

For he has his inheritance, his joy, the miraculous Bunch
of Grapes of his title, Christ the fruit of the vine Sion. It
would not be unlike Herbert to intend an ambiguity (and
through it to mock at his own inadequate conceptions) in
his first line's '*Joy*, I did lock thee up', i.e. both this capture
and possession of Christ *and* the locking up and denying
seven years ago of the unregenerate man's kind of 'joy'. But
this is not the only poem in which Joy and the soul's union
with Christ are identified, and it impoverishes the poem to
read its beginning as just one more of the complaints
against self-imposed repression of the natural man which
are found in Herbert by readers chiefly skilled in easy interpretations of 'The Collar'. 'I have *their* fruit', i.e. that of
the Jews, for whom he prays elsewhere 'that their sweet sap
might come again', with such self-accusatory vehemence—
'Poore nation, whose sweet sap and juice   Our cyens
have purloin'd' ('The Jews', p. 152). Sion is Noah's vine
(him of whom the whole earth was overspread, Gen. ix),
flourishing finally in the vine of Engaddy, traditionally the
Virgin in the liturgical and patristic allegorizations of the
Song of Solomon. Blessed be the God of the Old Testament,
but even more Christ who made out of the Old Dispensa-

tion the sweet wine of the New, the Wine of the Communion, that Blood pressed in the bitter pain of the Passion
from the God Himself who is the promised inheritance and
good store of grapes, to be a saving drink to all nations.

It is only possible to respond to the immediacy and richness with which such a poem can give shape to a man's
thoughts if we feel the full power of his figurative language,
as did his contemporaries. We do not have to know Isidore's allegorizing of the story of the grape cluster in Num.
xiii, nor Augustine's treatment in the Enarration on Ps.
viii,[4] nor any of the writers on Christian symbolism
that Herbert quite probably knew—Rabanus Maurus,
Hugo of St. Victor, Honorius Augustodunensis—to
whom Christ as *botrus* was a commonplace. But we do
have to read with a quickened inner eye, with an imagination made sensitive by images already stored in it. Let any
reader pick up a dozen among the scores of illustrated
Books of Hours now shored up in any library like the
British Museum or the Bodleian, with their thrice or four
times repeated series of types in woodcut vignettes down the
outer borders of each page; of this series the eleventh or
twelfth set portrays *Christ's Baptism* as Son of God in the
centre, the crossing of the *Red Sea* at the top, the huge *Bunch
of Grapes* carried on a pole by two men at the bottom (see
Plate V *b*). Or let such a reader encounter the same series
time and again in the editions of 'Queen Elizabeth's
Prayerbook' (STC 6428 ff.: 1569, '78, '81, '90, 1608)—
with the familiar great triangular cluster half the size of
the men carrying it, and the mute indication of equation with the Christ Baptized just above and with the
delivery from Pharaoh's enslavement just above that. Or

---

[4] Augustine calls Christ a cluster of grapes, like that brought hanging from
a staff 'crucified as it were', and makes the contrast between the sour juice of the
Old Testament (Christ drank the vinegar) and the sweet wine of the New.

let him recall coming upon even two or three of the vivid representations of Christ pressed in the wine-press of the Passion which Mâle puts forward in *L'art réligieux de la fin du moyen âge*; or let him think himself back to an England in which long series of the sets of types with accompanying verses could still be seen in the glass of Canterbury or St. Albans or in the paintings of Peterborough. Or let him take up copies of the popular *Biblia Pauperum* (from which the *Horae* series sprang; see Plate VI) with its cited Scriptural parallels, liturgical tags, and allegorical connexions. These additions to the mere pictured series relate the wells of salvation and purifying waters of Isa. xii and Ezek. xxxvi. 25 to the baptismal water and therefore, of course, to the water from Christ's side, relate Christ's delivery of us from original sin to the ancient delivery through the Red Sea (Herbert's 'sea of shame'), and relate the first-fetched grape-cluster from the Promised Land to that other crossing of the Jordan which is each Christian man's entrance into the kingdom of heaven, accomplished figuratively when he is signed with the water of baptism, and made possible by that cleansing 'fountain opened to the house of David' (Zech. xiii) which is equated with the death of the Christ.

Let a reader re-read Herbert's poem with these visual images and their clustered associations stored—however confusedly and faintly—in his memory, and he will experience freshly for himself the strength and power of the symbolical mode of writing. He will even be impatient with the poverty and blatancy of poetry which states emotions outright, as compared with the reticence with which Herbert states his self-disillusion by the ancient image—

> I did towards Canaan draw; but now I am
> Brought back to the Red sea, the sea of shame.

and with which he states his hope in

Then have we too our guardian fires and clouds;
　　Our Scripture⁄dew drops fast: . . .

　　　　I have their fruit and more. . . .
Ev'n God himself being pressed for my sake.

A reader so made sensitive to the full meaning of the
figures will perceive that there is another dimension to the
subject of this poem, beyond the mere conveyance of a
particular individual's emotion at a given time, that thin
subject with which modern readers have come to be con⁄
tent but which Herbert throws to one side with his 'A
single deed is small renown'. Herbert is seriously interested
in the idea that his case too is covered, taken count of, in an
eternally true series of events that preceded him in time; in
other words he reads history and biblical story as one great
web of metaphor. 'So now each Christian hath his journeys
spann'd'; God's 'ancient justice overflows *our* crimes'.
There is a kind of truth which includes what has not yet
happened. It is at this point that the poem widens to in⁄
clude us too, our Red Sea, our Canaan, our grape⁄cluster.
Herbert's grasp at the hope of disciplined and self⁄sacri⁄
ficing love even in the face of his own self⁄distrust is his
answer to the rebellion and the insufficiency of the single
suffering human creature; it is put in terms that would no
longer come naturally to us, but these are the necessities men
still cry out under and this the hope they still grasp at. *The
Waste Land* is not the only modern poem that voices both
this self⁄distrust and this hope, but it is one of the few that
has been able to create for readers symbols of a power equal
to those which Herbert found ready to his hand. Those
Herbert used are still sufficiently part of the living tissue of
Western culture to come alive to us too.

If with willingness to read the images for all they carry
we turn to 'The Agonie' (p. 37), we find Herbert writing

about one of the most vexing difficulties of a society in which information and techniques have outdistanced our understanding of the passions and motives of the human creature, and of their possibilities, for good or for bad. This is a fact not a problem; Herbert writes about the problem that lies behind the fact. About what makes the human will choose to be ignorant, of evil and of good, and whether it is incurable. Not, of course, in his first stanza, to whose statement of a situation we must retreat:

> Philosophers have measur'd mountains,
> Fathom'd the depths of seas, of states, and kings,
> Walk'd with a staffe to heav'n, and traced fountains:
> But there are two vast, spacious things,
> The which to measure it doth more behove:
> Yet few there are that sound them; Sinne and Love.

Herbert is concerned to 'sound' or 'measure'—to '*know* Sinne', in its workings what it is and does. He uses again the metaphor of the Press of the Passion; 'Sinne is *that presse and vice*, which forceth pain   To hunt his cruell food through ev'ry vein' (the pun on *vice* is possible but not necessary). But here the 'man so wrung with pains, that all his hair,   His skinne, his garments bloudie be' is the Christ of the Agony in the Garden, a traditionally fitting moment of the Passion to envisage here since part of Herbert's subject is the nature of evil as bared to the mind not as met in the body, the mind's agony when its depths are 'known', and man's continued responsibility for an agony that is never-ending as long as good shall be ground in the press of willed or allowed or wilful evil. Though he says that if we would know the nature of evil we must 'see' this, he is using a symbol, not a mere *icon* or picture. The reader's understanding of the agony of knowing, of the injustice, the blindness of bad men and the uncaring sleep of good ones, of the betrayal approaching and the unpitied pain, his understanding of all that is involved in that especial example is drawn upon *to make the concepts presented more subtle* —for Herbert is not occupied with making us sorry for Christ, he is defining sin: '*Who would know Sinne*, let him repair   Unto Mount Olivet.'

This use of a traditional image for conceptual refinement and depth is quite characteristic of Herbert, and also quite different from the daring intellectual neatness with which he is frequently credited. He can be apt when that is proper, but there is no smartness in Herbert's style, and the stop sounded here is rather that of a solemn and moving grief. He depends upon the associations that would be called to mind of Christ in the press or *torcular* of His Passion; this dependence is only possible for him because the image was a usual, not an unusual, one.

I mentioned above only very few of the channels by which this and related images came to be rooted in people's memories. Through long use they had ceased to be ingenious conceits and had become the natural language of deep feeling; for Herbert this would be not a sort of gratuitous extra merit in the images but the very reason why he should choose them. He is not the daring Metaphysical innovator wittily joining the lowly press to the exalted idea of Christ, but the poet choosing familiar and moving language, when he chooses to write with the very tone and imagery of a prayer known to hundreds of Englishmen, one of that famous set known as *The fifteen Oes*. I quote from it as printed by Caxton in the little illustrated book with that title, but these 'prayers of St. Bridget' even appear in the several-times-printed 'Queen Elizabeth's Prayerbook' of 1578 ff.,[5] and the set had been printed in very many *Horae* and Primers.

[5] The 1578 *Book of Christian Prayers* (STC *s.n.* R. Day) is conveniently accessible in the Parker Society reprint (ed. W. K. Clay, *Private Prayers . . . the*

O Blessed Jhesu verai and true plenteuous vyne· Have mynde of thy passion & habundaunt shedynge of blode / that thou sheddest most plenteuously, as yf it had be threst out of a rype clustre of grapes. Whan they pressed thy blessid body as a ripe clustre upon the pressour of the crosse / And yave us drynke both blode and water out of thy body. . . .

It would be a mistake to suppose that the hundreds of copies of laymen's devotional books like the *Horae* or Primer went out of use, even did we not realize that such sets of prayers continued to reappear elsewhere, in Becon's *Pomander of prayer*, for instance. This image, like many, cannot have been other than familiar.

For symbols, the popularity of books fixing such images in the *visual* memory is especially pertinent. The two great popular compendia whence iconographical conventions of this kind were drawn in the late Middle Ages and early Renaissance are the *Biblia Pauperum* and the *Speculum humanae salvationis*; the *Speculum* makes even more vivid use than the *BP* of the patristic and devotional symbol of Christ as the grapes pressed in the torment of the Passion to make the drink of salvation. Like the *BP*, this second text came out as one of the early block-books with which studies of the history of printing and of book-illustration have made us familiar; like it, the *Speculum* was spread about in a very great number of manuscripts widely distributed in the different countries of Europe; like it, the text was translated (into German prose and verse, Dutch, French prose and verse, English verse, Czech) and widely reprinted. Moreover, like the *BP*, the *Speculum* developed liturgical connexions which ensured the carrying on of the full tradi-

Reign of Queen Elizabeth, Cambridge, 1851; see p. 512). The reprint reproduces the marginal scriptural tags but not the woodcut series of types that they accompanied, which I mentioned earlier; these may be picked up in a Victorian BCP which copies this series and other sets of 1578 ff., including the Dance of Death (one e.g. of 1863, London: Bickers and Bush).

tion with all its symbolic force. As the *Biblia Pauperum* picture-series was literally broadcast through its use in Books of Hours, with scriptural references and liturgical tags preserved even in the Protestant 'Queen Elizabeth's Prayerbook', so the woodcuts and text of the *Speculum* series were attached to the epistles and gospels for the church year, appearing thus many times in German and thence in French amplified versions.[6] Each of the forty-odd members of the typological series in the *Speculum* provides four pictures —three Old Testament types and a New Testament antitype—instead of the three of the *BP*. The wine-press conceit appears twice: the first time in an explanation of the spiritual meaning of the vine of Pharaoh's butler's dream, which is a type of the Nativity, as are also the flowering rod of Aaron and the Tiburtine sibyl's vision of a virgin and child (the fourth picture is often drawn from legend). Mankind had suffered long, at last a vine Jesus sprang of the earth Mary (when Christ was born the vines of Engaddy flourished), and the wine of Christ's blood having been pressed in the Cross, on the third day was man's freedom sealed. The other appearance of the conceit in the *Speculum* is in connexion with the *botrus* or miraculous grape-bunch carried huge and triangular upon its pole as we are accustomed to see it.

Since the pictured anti-type in the *Speculum* set is Christ carrying His Cross, the two other types being little Isaac with the wood for his own sacrifice and the slaying of the

[6] The French translation which parallels the German of Basle 1476 appears in Lyons editions of 1478, '79, '82, '83, '88, '93; moreover, texts which appeared under such imprints as Zainer and Vérard were not obscure books, and names of Renaissance collectors are found on our copies (e.g. the British Museum copy of Lyons 1493 is a Lumley book). The iconographical tradition in the *BP* and the *Speculum* shows that odd constancy which always surprises a modern, unaccustomed to 'reading' pictorial details as elements of meaning. The many manuscripts I have seen are not typically handsome ones, serving often no doubt as handbooks of designs.

vineyard-owner's son, the equation between miraculous grape-cluster and sacrificed Son of God is even more sharply indicated pictorially. (See Plates VII, VIII *a*, and see frontispiece for parallels with other types of the Cross: Brazen Serpent, Tau, and the widow of Sarepta with her sticks.) One needs to see but a few of the many versions to find that it is quite impossible to see the grape-cluster without thinking of the Passion, or to think of Isaac without seeing Christ carrying His Cross. A hundred rhymed lines accompany each set of pictures, making up a text which, unlike the *Biblia Pauperum*, had importance for itself and sometimes appeared unillustrated.[7] The text connects the grape-bunch, as Herbert does, with the vine which figures forth the nation of Israel, the wine-press, and the sacrificial blood; we are reminded of Herbert's 'the taste of mine inheritance' when it says that as the grape-cluster showed Israel the fruitfulness of the Promised Land, so by Christ we know of the sweetness of celestial joys to come.

As we realize the full significance of Herbert's 'their' and 'my' fruit, we see that the poem cannot be confined within

[7] This and a fifteenth-century French translation may be read in the edition by J. Lutz and P. Perdrizet (see the Note on accessibility of materials to early readers, at the end of this book); it lists some 200 manuscripts and many editions and translations, and discusses some of the appearances of this typological series in art. The *Bible moralisée* MSS. offer another such series; on too grandiose a scale to be widespread, its illuminations show how firm were the conventions for representation of the grape-cluster, Samson's gates, Christ's side-wounding and Eve's creation, and other parallels with Herbert. But I keep to very widely diffused texts, which saw print. Otherwise I should cite from the *Pictor in carmine*, a thirteenth-century handbook, probably English in provenance, specifically designed to 'influence painters in churches', and citing the Canaanitish grape-bunch as a type of the Crucifixion, along with 137 other groups of conventional parallels, many of them also in Herbert (Bodl. MS. Rawl. A 425 and others; described by M. R. James in Cambr. Antiq. Soc. *Proceedings*, vii. 58 ff; see above, p. 55n.). In connexion with these seemingly obscure medieval texts we have to remember two things: that there *was* wide diffusion of allegorical commentaries like that of Hugo de S. Charo, which was a source for the *Bible moralisée* according to its editor A. de Laborde; and that the paintings, glass, &c., which were thus 'influenced' did remain to be seen by later writers.

the category of spiritual autobiography. Christ the cluster, as the inheritance of the Gentiles, Love not Law as the final fruit of the vine, is one part of his subject in 'The Bunch of Grapes'. The two men who carry the bunch between them on the pole, one preceding the other, are frequently explained as the Jews and the Gentiles.[8]

This is not a tangential point. Herbert is almost as preoccupied with the relation between the Old Dispensation and the New as are the typological materials and the allegorical glosses which he so often echoes; considerations of God as Law or rigorous Justice and God as Love are thematic not haphazard in his work, and to recognize this theme is to become aware of a unity in the whole body of his poetry which Herbert did not live to perfect but which is an aesthetic satisfaction to anyone who reads him whole. This is a book about Ecclesia, and her great Type, Synagogue, is as ever-present here as she had been in presentations of Ecclesia in other forms of symbolic Christian art.

Poem after poem is clarified by this realization of an underlying theme. It is in 'Whitsunday', in most of the Priesthood poems, in 'Aaron', 'The Jews', 'Sion', the 'Jordan' poems. We see, for example, that the great ancient contrast has produced a poem of penitence in 'The Jews' (p. 152), which again has the vine conceit, and that it is probably a Good Friday poem, written for the day when the Church as one body had always offered her corporate prayer for the Jews, in imitation of Christ's on the Cross. There is no suspicion of self-righteousness in Herbert's handling of the old theme.

> Oh that my prayers! mine, alas!
> Oh that some Angel might a trumpet sound;

---

[8] This explanation in Isidore (on the book of Num.) and Rabanus Maurus was spread through citation in the *Glossa ordinaria*; see also Mâle, *L'Art relig. du xiiie siècle*, bk. iv, ch. 1.

> At which the Church falling upon her face
> Should crie so loud, untill the trump were drown'd,
> And by that crie of her deare Lord obtain,
>   That your sweet sap might come again!

The tone in his self-correction—'. . . *mine*, alas!'—is an example of that humility which gives such endearing sweetness to Herbert's voice that it is not possible to read the poet without loving the man. Herbert believes his symbols; he believes that Ecclesia's eyes were opened to a revelation of Heavenly Love, and that it was a true revelation. His humility does not take the easy shape we have so conveniently found for that virtue, a tentativeness directed towards bodies of ideas, at a safe remove from our own selves; he is humble in the more difficult way of perceiving his own unworthiness as an exponent of the truth he believes. Consequently the poem really breathes that spirit of unassertive *caritas* which Herbert happened to think was historically the peculiar contribution of Christianity. His history can be found mistaken, his Church proved insufficient, his Angel a delusion—the poem remains a prayer for the universal victory of that spirit. The irony of our 'purloined' salvation is emphasized by the use of the symbol of Israel as the vine whose 'sweet sap and juice' the Gentiles got, all undeserving, 'by the Apostles sluce'. The figurative reference to the wounded Christ of the Passion and the other figures (of the preacher as trumpet, of Ecclesia as undeserving petitioner) make the poem primarily an expression of penitent humility in the possession of unmerited gains got by others' loss; we read about an attitude of mind, not about a single historical situation.

Bearing in mind the centrality for Herbert of the Christian idea of the new Ecclesia built in the hearts of the faithful, we see a deeper meaning in 'Sion' (p. 106), which is

a poem ostensibly about Solomon's temple, really about
Zion the faithful people or Church of God—at any time.
Herbert writes of God's quitting of his 'ancient claim' of
external rite and Law for a temple within the human heart
(for a 'frame and fabrick all within', a Church made by
Christ as indwelling Love); he writes of how this has
brought a new danger bred of a new necessity. That necessity is constant vitality of individual spiritual life. When
the Church is built in this new place God's 'Architecture
meets with sinne'. The image which carries the meaning
most climactically and concisely is one we should not even
recognize without an informed acquaintance with Christian symbolism: 'All Solomons sea of brasse and world of
stone   Is not so deare to thee as one good grone.' 'Solomons sea of brasse' (1 Kings vii. 23) is not simply an
illustrative example of magnificent pomp; it refers to the
ornate brass laver or 'sea', standing upon the twelve oxen,
which had become familiar as a prefiguring of Christian
baptism and of the twelve apostles (e.g. *Glossa ordinaria*,
from Bede). As so often, its difference from the Christian
anti-type which it prefigures is that between letter and spirit
(the chief concern of Herbert's 'Sion'). The *Speculum
humanae salvationis*, picturing the sea of brass in juxtaposition
to Christ's baptism by John with the new 'baptism of
repentance', emphasizes this difference by telling how John
called the Pharisees a generation of vipers because they
would approach baptism without contrition; this is a proper commentary upon Herbert's 'All Solomons sea of
brasse and world of stone   Is not so deare to thee as one
good grone'. Pictures in the *Speculum* (see Plates IX *a*, *b*,
X *a*) as usual nail down the correspondence with a memor-
able visual image; the oxen (apostles) are often diverting.
The other two types of baptism—which, of course, is the
act of entrance into the Church spiritually conceived—are

the Ark carried through the divided Jordan, and Naaman purified of his leprosy by bathing in Jordan's waters.

These types, as I shall show later, are related not simply to images in Herbert but to a discernible group of poems, of which the two puzzlingly entitled 'Jordan' are chief and key. This group is involved with a whole complex of Herbert's ideas about sacred and profane love, and when we examine these poems in connexion with their basis in Christian symbolism we shall come upon certain other results of Herbert's persistent preoccupation with the New Dispensation and with its nature, its demands, and its rewards. Just here it is apposite only to remind ourselves that the theme of the section called 'The Church', like that of any treatment of Ecclesia, is Love.

Too much has been made of the Herbert who had inner conflicts over giving up the life of the world and the flesh to go into orders; the theme of any symbolic treatment of the love of the soul for Christ, of the Church for the Bridegroom, is the wooing of that soul to gradual submission. The multitudinous other treatments of this theme by Herbert's predecessors would seem 'personal' and 'deeply felt' too, if we were sufficiently educated in the tradition they represent to read them properly. The theme is personal and sharply realized in its very nature. Herbert's poetry is personal for the same reason that it is Christocentric; the central principle of life as he in his person has been able with pain to discover it is self-abnegating love. No man discovers this without pain, most of us will never do more than hear about it, and none of us perhaps knows quite what to do with such a principle in the context of present thinking. Although neither the pain nor the discovery is confined to the Christian religion, it is yet a necessity of history that Herbert should have phrased them in the terms and symbols of that tradition in England in the 1620's. It should be obvious against this background that his poetry does not concern itself so intimately with the Church because Herbert was a cleric. He is supremely interested in something which he in his historical context would perforce see as 'manifested' to Ecclesia and only 'prefigured' to all the world beside—the new dispensation of Love (*caritas*, *agape*) revealed in Christ as sacrifice for men. He writes about his attempts to find out what *caritas* is and relate himself, purged of self-will, to it; his partial success is more important poetically, though it is more alien ground to us, than his difficulties.

The final stanza of 'The Agonie' (p. 37) says something of all this, as we can see when we return to the poem after such a review of the reverberations of meaning awakened by the use of these symbols. Seeing Sin and Love as deeper mysteries than those uncovered by the natural philosophers who measure mountains and walk with their staves to heaven, Herbert's characteristic way of 'sounding' the depths of these mysteries is to reveal their nature in images rather than to discuss it. He is not obscurantist, and his piety is not of the kind that denies the validity of the many and various kinds of human knowledge; this is not a pietistic poem, and they are not the pious thinkers in our own world who make a substantially similar answer to Herbert's inquiry concerning the mode of knowing those areas of reality which include values, motivation, the 'good' and 'bad' springs of human behaviour. Some things are to be known only by apprehending the workings of them. And only an awakened imagination apprehends and recognizes, for experience can be blind as a bat and empty as a house never lived in. He has by a symbol shown what evil looks like when it is at work; now he would by a symbol set forth what he thinks can defeat it. Would you know what love is? Experience it, he says; taste of it in its essential

form, when it was for once revealed pure, 'assay' especially
that real but mysterious element in it which relates it to
what we call sacrifice.

> Who knows not Love, let him assay
> And taste that juice, which on the crosse a pike
> Did set again abroach; then let him say
> If ever he did taste the like.
> Love is that liquor sweet and most divine,
> Which my God feels as bloud; but I, as wine.

Herbert's belief in an actual revelation of self-immolating
'heavenly' love as a new principle for the moral life is
obvious here; but as usual it is the use of the symbol rather
than of more direct statements about the Christian dispensation which makes the poem mean something even outside
the domain of believed Christian dogma. Herbert would
have us learn the essential nature of some important 'un-
measured' aspects of reality by tasting the quality of them
in their operation. Both myth and poetry assist to this kind
of knowing. Herbert's great instrument is the first; his
poems offer us the instrument of the second.

Although it is in figures that poetry catches and holds
the very beating of the naked thinking heart, figures can be
a hindrance more than a help if they are too difficult to
enter, too obtrusive. This is something which is only partially under the poet's control. The images of 'The Agonie',
for example, are radical and to us surprising; but they are
not audacious, they are conventional—and when we read
Herbert's poems without knowing this we take away from
them the quietness which is part of their power. Christ as
the tun of wine, broached for our drinking, is one of the
numerous variants on the grapes-and-wine-press theme.
An Easter sequence of Adam of St. Victor's follows up
the conceit of the pressed grape-cluster with almost the

same metaphor: *Saccus scissus et pertusus.*[9] A *saccus* was both a purse and a bag for straining wine through; Herbert uses a similar figure in 'The Bag', where the wounded Christ is Himself the bag, with an open place 'very near his heart' wherein he will carry the requests of any to His Father (p. 151). In their setting Herbert's images, like the medieval ones, are potent and direct; they are not naïve and they are not over-ingenious; they are simply the natural flowering of symbolic writing. Adam of St. Victor turns his *saccus* into *soccus glorie*; Herbert's post-bag to which anything may be conveyed with a mere sigh shows a similar operation of the images. They do not offend (are not merely and trivially fanciful) because they stay consistently symbolic, and the fact that they do this is their patent of safe-conduct in a later world that may not believe in the same letter but still faces the problems of guilt and redemption which the symbols dealt with. We have, of course, to accustom ourselves to seeing all the details (of 'The Bag', for example) in their symbolic dimension—the God that descended 'undressing all the way', that had 'new clothes a making here below' (i.e. the coat of flesh: *Humanitas Christi*, that was to be so torn and riven), the inn where he paid with his life the score for all the guests, and the rest of the details. Once we are thus accustomed we do not see an ingeniously allegorical narrative of the incarnation and atonement but see within that the real theme of the poem, Herbert's hopeful and

---

[9] This sequence, *Ecce dies celebris*, was printed as Adam's in Clichtoveus's study of the poetry of the liturgy; as the most outstanding of such studies, his *Elucidatorium Ecclesiasticum* was very likely known to Herbert, a student of liturgy and himself a writer of Christian Latin poetry on similar subjects. The point is not essential; what is important is how many men of the Renaissance were interested to study and to praise medieval poetry which helped to give such images currency. See the Note on accessibility of materials, at the end of the book. Durandus's often-printed *Rationale* (see the same Note) uses the wine-press conceit in his sections on Holy Wednesday and Thursday in connexion with the image of one-coming-in-dyed-garments-from-Bozrah, discussed by Hutchinson in the essay cited n. 17 of Part I above.

joyful conception of the nature of love as the very loss of the self in sympathetic identification with that which is loved.

The same sort of images, proliferated from a publicly accepted and clear and natural symbol, show in 'Divinitie' (p. 134). Christ is that 'Wisdome', *Sapientia Patris*, which 'first broacht the wine' of Heavenly Love, his blood; could he not, if he wished, 'have thicken'd it with definitions'?

And jagg'd his seamlesse coat, had that been fine,
With curious questions and divisions?

Christ's garment is the type of love and hence of unity in the Church. But the doctrine which was the only divinity he taught was not 'fine' or subtle like that knowledge by which man has sought to order both heavens; it was obscure not as fine-drawn things but as profound things are obscure; consisted only of those 'dark instructions', 'dark as day': *Love God, and love your neighbour.* These are 'Gordian knots'; this is not the kind of 'divinity' the defining mind can cut and carve, yet such wisdom can make an orderly harmony of man's universe. 'Then burn thy Epicycles, foolish man', those smaller circles into which man has mapped out both the physical and the spiritual heavens; *this* wisdom is the great all-encompassing circle along whose circumference the centres of the others move, this love is an ordering principle though the order is one we can only taste not define, just as we are told inscrutably that God's love is blood we are to 'take for wine'. Again, this is not an obscurantist poem, written to discredit the natural and moral philosopher's rational modes of ordering reality, though its beginning and ending might lead us to think so. The positive core of the poem is a definition—in symbols—of 'Divinitie' (the title is a pun); it is by his symbols that Herbert indicates what this discipline involves, this hard study of an ordering principle beyond the competence of the defining reason. This would be to us just one more of those poems telling us to have faith and not think, unless we have what Herbert expects us to have, a quick and unselfconscious recognition of the broached wine and the garment as symbols of that kind of love which is the very nature of the divine in action. It is typical of a symbolic image that the details into which it breaks are physical or sensuous (the *thickening*, the ornamental *jaggings* and piec- ings), and would seem fanciful, quaint, and more ingenious than moving, if not seen instantly *as* what they signify. Here the danger we avert by knowing more is that of imposing upon poems a tone that does not belong to them at all.

In the much simpler 'Good Friday' (p. 38) it is not the tone which is easy to miss but certain delicately suggested complexities of idea; without intellectual pith such devo- tional poetry can be offensively limp. The poem ends as a prayer but begins as a proper *meditatio*: 'How shall I measure out thy bloud?' count thy griefs, number thy woes? Its two originally separate parts were probably combined because each deals with the way in which sorrowing love, by possessing the heart, is a 'cure' for sin. Herbert has a set of comparisons for the innumerableness of Christ's griefs: his numberless foes, the stars (but *one* showed his *first* breath), the falling leaves, ending with 'Or can not leaves, but fruit, be signe   Of the true vine?' These would be flat and lifeless mere comparisons if the Epiphany star did not become Christ as *sol justitiae*, 'my sunne', and if the vine image did not convey two ideas at once and cause the turn in the thought from meditation to resolve: Christ the vine's Good Friday fruit, man no scion of the true vine if he bears no fruit. The second half begins:

> Since bloud is fittest, Lord, to write
> Thy sorrows in, and bloudie fight;
> My heart hath store, write there, where in
> One box doth lie both ink and sinne:

The connexions between *blood* and *love* (familiar also in the physiology and psychology of the day) are never far away in images such as this traditional medieval one;[10] without them Herbert's line about the ink would read as trivial to the point of silliness.

A seeming over-cleverness and toy-like triviality renders poems like 'Love-joy' (p. 116) suspect to us; though all untrivial poems are not good ones at least this obstacle to reading disappears against such a background as that outlined in these pages.

> As on a window late I cast mine eye,
> I saw a vine drop grapes with *J* and *C*
> Anneal'd on every bunch. One standing by
> Ask'd what it meant. I, who am never loth
> To spend my judgement, said, It seem'd to me
> To be the bodie and the letters both
> Of *Joy* and *Charitie*. Sir, you have not miss'd,
> The man reply'd; It figures *JESUS CHRIST*.

For one thing, this is one of the kind of 'occasional' poems, with the conversational and casual tone proper to such pieces; it is a poem of the kind of Yeats's 'Stream and Sun

---

[10] The write-in-the-heart-with-blood image is in the *Fifteen Oes*. A variant forms the base of a poem still more alien to our taste, 'Jesu', p. 112. It occurs in liturgy, hymns, lyrics, but most familiarly in meditation literature in prose and verse (Pseudo-Augustine, St. Bernard), and Herbert's connexion with the Instruments of the Passion is usual. See Carleton Brown's notes to a 14th-cent. lyric (xiv: 91) built on the pattern of this repeated 'write . . . write . . . write'; for example:

> Write up-on my hert boke
> Thy faire & swete lovely loke, . . .
> Write the strokes with hameres stout
> With the blood rennynge a-bowt; . . .
> And with that blode write thou so ofte,
> Myn hard hert til hit be softe.

This variant of writing-in-the-stony-heart is used by Herbert in 'The Sinner' p. 38, and in 'Sepulchre', p. 40, where appears another traditional connexion—with the O.T. type of the 'Law . . . writ in stone' (common type and contrast for Pentecost; see, for example, *Biblia Pauperum*). Emblem-writing shares in these traditions.

at Glendalough' or 'Coole and Ballylee, 1931' or Donne's 'A Jeat Ring sent'. For Herbert quite probably did see Christ the Grape-bunch in an actual old window, put up with the precise intention of 'figuring Jesus Christ', like the one once at St. Albans, paralleling the grapes, the Cross-carrying and Isaac.[11] *Anneal'd* is very exact; so is the contrast between 'bodie' (embodied manifestation) and 'letters', with the wit of a double reference in the first. Stained glass is the art which made the most extensive use of typological series, except for the book-illustrations such as those I have mentioned. Although the pun on the initial letters of *Gaudium* and *Caritas* in English is Herbert's own, it is necessary to be aware of the familiar connexion of the Grapes with the Baptism and with the Crucifixion, supreme examples of *Joy* (liberation from the Egyptian captivity, *fons vitae*, marriage of Christ with the Soul, with the Church), and of *Love* (sacrificed on the Cross for man). Perhaps the only important thing to add about this poem is that Christ as the grapes pressed in the wine-press of the Passion is almost always connected not with sorrow but with joy. He is *potus laetitiae*. Mary Magdalene, who typifies the sinner's realization of his need to repent, is the sorrowful symbol, as myrrh is the bitter and painful one. But the blood of the Crucifixion, in an image using wine, is a wine of gladness. 'Botrus pro laetitia ponitur', says Honorius, describing the grape-cluster and wine-press image in an exposition of Canticles i. 13, another favourite connexion for it.

[11] Dugdale prints the verses accompanying the sets of types in the now destroyed St. Albans windows; but see M. R. James in Cambr. Antiq. Soc. *Proceedings*, vii. 31–69 and ix. 178–94, on various appearances. The Canterbury glass, still visible in Herbert's day and carefully described by Wm. Somner in *Antiq. of Cant.*, London, 1640, has many other parallels with Herbert—Melchisedec: Lord's Supper: manna; Baptism: Naaman; Side-wounding: Eve's creation; Joseph: Christ; Samson's gates, &c. I do not oftener mention the full and striking 16th-cent. series at King's College because these present but *two* paralleled scenes; they use parallels from both the *Speculum* and the *Biblia Pauperum-Horae* sets.

I have tried, by examining this group of poems using images and ideas that cluster around a certain ancient symbol for Christ, to demonstrate the only two important points I have to make: that symbols are a language which enables poems to be permanently valid, and that if we will learn the language, which is in some cases an archaic and difficult one, we shall not mistake the poet's tone of voice but accurately take his meanings even across intervening centuries.

We shall also be saved some errors concerning the nature of poetry, and Metaphysical poetry in particular, which ultimately work to cut us off from enjoyment of the whole long tradition of poetic writing. Spenser is, of course, the most notable example of a great poet all but lost to modern readers with a fair degree of critical sophistication. I have spoken of the modern need to complement a rationally discursive, empirical world-view with that kind of approach to the real which sees into it, and presents it, through metaphor and symbol. Modern poets, peculiarly aware of this need and trying to practise this approach, made no mistake when they seized upon Metaphysical poets as exemplars. But we have all busied ourselves with setting off the part instead of seeing the whole, in not perceiving that Metaphysical wit and concord of unlikes in an image is precisely the operation, much condensed, of the old (and maligned) allegorical mode of writing. The metaphorical unit is larger and the treatment almost casually spacious in the Saturn and Mars of the *Knight's Tale* or in the *Mutability Cantos*, as compared with the pin-point of Donne's compass image or lecture on a shadow, or Herbert's rose with its root ever in the grave; and a Donne uses fewer traditional and openly known metaphors (symbols) than a Herbert, so that it is harder to see how traditionally they serve their immemorial purpose of peering into meanings at the heart of things. Yet to miss this similarity between the Metaphysicals and other great poets is to seize upon the husk and let the kernel drop. The homely or the seemingly fanciful expansion of a basic 'conceit' (concept, quite truly), the proliferation of precise concrete particulars or sensuous physical details—these are inevitable elements in symbolic writing, for they are how it functions. They appear in this form or in that in all eras when insight into truth through the telescope of metaphor has been commonly and confidently practised; we cheat ourselves of what we most need to know if we do not recognize a telescope whenever we see one.

Certain historical eras have been especially competent in this mode of approach to reality. The medieval period stands out in this respect, largely perhaps because of the medieval Christian Church; but it is clear from late classi-cal and medieval uses of classical myth or from medieval cosmology that I speak of a habit of the mind, not of a Christian world-view. Spenser had not lost the habit of mind, and both Herbert's pulley and collar and Donne's making a symbol of an Elizabeth Drury are directly in the stream of tradition which flowed from the Middle Ages through Spenser and the sixteenth century. Writers in this tradition see the world as a complex of meanings or values —seen pure, in their essence, as we do see the 'meaning' in metaphors, apprehended and appreciated rather than demonstrated and utilized; writing in this tradition shows this world in images. No one states this power of poetry more clearly than Sidney; and, of course, it did not get lost, poetry did not die.

But the habit of mind lost caste, and *readers*, rather than poets, lost the knack of it, in a world that expected religion to be science and poetry to be the *literal* truth (both of them expectations naturally doomed to disappointment). The earlier mode of approach to reality, apprehending truth directly, through figure, has its limitations and its excesses like any other. Men in the Middle Ages or the sixteenth century looked at the world and saw only part of it, just as we do. But in our present lopsidedness it probably behoves us to learn wherever we can. Either the historian of science or the Grail Knight can tell us we shall not learn until we ask the right question; a good many of the typical questions we ask of poetry are designed only to lead us again to what we already know. We need to ask of a Metaphysical poem how its metaphors operate to provide insight, which is a thing its writer had learned from predecessors most subtly skilled therein, and not what peculiar tricks of technique and modernities of temper it exhibits. The way a poem is written inescapably constitutes some thinking mind's read⁄ing of life, and the secret of Metaphysical wit lies in a reading of life (of the nature of truth and of knowledge) inherited through at least the ten or twelve preceding centuries.

This is an observation about literary *form*. But its truth comes out with special clarity in religious poems because not only the attitude of mind but the actual metaphors themselves are traditional. This last is true of Donne's reli⁄gious poems as well as of Herbert's; the *Corona* is so full of echoes to an ear acquainted with the liturgy, and the Holy Sonnets and the other Divine Poems are so full of ancient conceits, that the question 'what makes these so truly John Donne's?' becomes a very provocative one. I shall introduce occasional parallel examples from Donne, now that the ground has been cleared for a review of Herbert's many and various traditional metaphors. Both wrote short poems, and were devotional poets in a way their predecessors were not (except Southwell, a Catholic), both escaped an earlier— and a later—Protestant hesitancy to make striking use of 'Papistical' symbolism, and both had reason to know parti⁄

cularly well traditions which after all had remained most alive in devotional, liturgical, or other religious materials. But I shall leave proper treatment of Donne for a later essay elsewhere and emphasize Herbert, since he wrote no *libertin* love poems to catch the ear of the general and since his churchly subject-matter has been more of an obstacle to recognition of the great beauty of his poetry. To be sure, six or seven of his poems have had all or more than their due. We have liked him in spite of ourselves—or rather in spite of himself and for a rather narrow little list of things in him that seemed like ourselves. Scarcely a poem of Herbert's lacks the witty quality, the tension, the apparent mingling of homeliness with sublimity, the surprise and shock, which currently give us such special pleasure and which we know in our own poets. It is all the more important to show the traditional nature of many of his conceits, even those unimportant ones which he lets fall by the way. This will amount to a demonstration of likenesses between the 'Metaphysical' manner and the great religious and secular allegorical tradition, regnant for centuries, upon which it was nourished—which is not just a point of literary history but a point about one of poetry's most valuable ways of looking at the world, that is, one of her greatest formal discoveries. I hope it may also show that a good poet tells us most when we make every effort to let him speak in his own voice.

§2. *Wit*

Here we rejoin the second of what I called above my only two important points. This point (which touches the hotly contested modern critical issues of whether historical knowledge is ever aesthetically necessary, and of 'what' and 'where' a poem is) was suggested but scarcely proved; it concerned the relation between knowledge of symbols and the tone we read in, and between tone and meaning. Herbert is acute, original, and apt; he is not self-consciously clever, fond of daring innovations, or playfully neat. Partly because of the picture-poems, 'The Altar' and 'Easter-wings', he is often thought of as a writer who liked to perform stunts or toy with oddities. It is important to notice some of the many cases in which the similitudes or details that seem to us most wittily novel, 'Metaphysical', baroque, or far-fetchedly ingenious are either outright conventions in traditional allegorical materials, or take their spring from such inherited symbols. Not all of these have the importance and thematic force of symbols, and in the group of examples which follows I include images, locutions, conceits, or notions, generally without attempting to show their interconnexions or the fructifying effect of such inheritances in the development of whole poems.

One of the most striking of Herbert's conceits is this whole poem (p. 77):

$$Ana\text{-}\begin{Bmatrix} MARY \\ ARMY \end{Bmatrix}gram.$$

How well her name an *Army* doth present,
In whom the *Lord of Hosts* did pitch his tent!

Two traditional associations made this poem both less startling and more enjoyable to its writer and its first readers than to us. The first is the image of an army with banners for the Virgin Mary, in biblical commentary, in the liturgy of many of her feasts, and in the motets which a person knowledgeable about church-music would know. The image comes from Song of Solomon vi, where it occurs twice; the motet text reads (e.g. see Palestrina's four or five settings, both *Pulchra es* and *Quae est ista quae progreditur*): 'Pulchra es, o Maria virgo, suavis et decora, terribilis ut castrorum

acies ordinata . . .' ('terrible as an army with banners').[12]
Allegories of the Song of Solomon, in commentary and in
famous writers' treatises, were thoroughly familiar in this
century; the Virgin is a type of Ecclesia, and, of course, in
the King James version these verses are interpreted as per-
taining to the Church alone. The image attained special
currency from its repeated use as antiphon and *capitulum* in
the Small Office (said Saturdays) of the Virgin Mary,
appearing therefore repeatedly in the copies of *Horae* to be
found everywhere. Of course, it appears in many less popu-
larly known contexts, in the liturgy, in Adam of St. Victor's sequence *Jerusalem et Sion filiae* (of Ecclesia), and in
very many Marian poems—and if we hesitate to believe that
Herbert, a Protestant, knew such poems, we must confront
the fact that this of his own is a typical one. The anagram-
matic point, possible only in English, is (to my knowledge)
Herbert's own; but it would not be easy for even an ill-read
seventeenth-century Anglican cleric to avoid thinking of
Mary and Army as belonging together, and, moreover, to
think of that Army as 'The Church Militant' *as well as*
Mary. I wish I knew how many of my readers had caught
on first reading the whole new spread of meaning which
this double operation of the metaphor gives to a poem that
is not so tiny after all—Herbert is constantly preoccupied
with how the Lord of Hosts has 'pitched his tent' in the
hearts of his *familia*, and Mary is the great allegory of that
descent and union. The last line is not only, in other words,
a reference to the event of the Incarnation, but to the
Incarnation as itself a great metaphor.

[12] In polyphonic music the phrase in question is emphasized by repetition
very many times in the different voices, and any musician knows how such
repeated images become the familiar furniture of the mind. I have spoken
earlier of Herbert's twice-a-week practising of church-music in a singing-
group, and his long Cambridge years were spent in a place far richer in sacred
music and musicians than Salisbury.

It is also, of course, a reference to the Incarnation as an event, and in most conventional terms, novel and witty as they may seem to us. They are wittier than we see. 'Pitched his *tent*' has for us various unsuitable reverberations; for Herbert it held pretty certainly the different and much deeper implications of some common Vulgate phrase like 'extendit *tabernaculum* suum', which it translates. 'Pitched his *tent* in' appears a dozen times as the King James translation of '. . . tabernaculum'. Durandus explicitly glosses *tabernaculum* as 'tent' or 'womb of Mary'.[13] 'In sole posuit tabernaculum suum' begins that verse of Ps. 19 whose continuing image, the Bridegroom issuing from his chamber exulting as a strong man to run a race, is so persistently used of Nativity and Epiphany in all Christian literature (partly because it was in a *Horae* Matins psalm). The Virgin (and the Church) as tabernacle of the Deity is implicated with a whole web of symbolism, and this is the second of the two traditional associations which illuminate the poem's meaning as well as its origin.

Mary is commonly in hymns, sequences, antiphons called the tabernacle of God; she is the *ark*, in whom is 'closed' the manna or Christ the bread of life, she is the *urna aurea*, shining golden with virtue within and without, the ark of God's testament, holding Love as the old ark had held the Tables of the Law, holding the new flowering Rod that displaced 'Aaron's yerde', she is the very candelabra, Christ's bright lantern, containing the ineffable brilliance of the *sol justitiae*. These I cite for convenience from that mine of commonplaces the *Speculum humanae salva-*

---

[13] Durandus's *Rationale* says in treating of the Assumption of the Virgin (15 Aug.) that the lesson for that day, from Ecclus. xxiv, including 'et qui creavit me, requievit in tabernaculo meo' means 'Et mon créateur s'est reposé dans mon tabernacle *ou ma tente, c'est à dire dans mon sein*' (Bk. vii, tr. Barthélemy). This is a book we shall notice more particularly presently, but see the Note on 17th-cent. accessibility of such materials.

tionis (on the Presentation, on the First Joy of the B.V.M.). The gilded box⁄like pictures, conventional reliquary⁄like representations of the ark of the tabernacle, remind us that Herbert also symbolizes the Incarnation by a 'box' ('Un⁄ gratefulnesse', p. 82):

> Thou hast but two rare cabinets full of treasure,
> The *Trinitie*, and *Incarnation*:
> Thou hast unlockt them both,
> And made them jewels to betroth
> The work of thy creation
> Unto thy self in everlasting pleasure.

It is Herbert's characteristically original turn to say further that the *second* 'box we know;   For we have all of us just such another', in our own 'poore cabinet of bone'—though that heart in which God should be we make rather into sin's 'box'. But both this and the quoted stanza must be read with the ark: Incarnation and *ecclesia*: *archa* symbols in mind, as well as the wedding of a Christian soul to God. At least the poem is richer read so, and its author probably intended the richness, since he and his audience must have known the symbols.

The same holds for two other Herbert images which are connected with the symbolism of tabernacle (with its O.T. contents, especially the Law) taken as a type of Church, soul, or Virgin (ark holding Love, Christ). The first, in 'Sepulchre', is slight, and uses another convention also, but typifies the several Love⁄templed⁄in⁄the⁄heart images: 'And as of old the Law . . . Was writ in stone; so thou, which also art   The letter of the word, find'st no fit heart   To hold thee' (all are stone; p. 40). More subtle is 'O rack me not to such a vast extent; . . . The world's too little *for thy tent*,   A grave too big for me' ('The Temper, 1', p. 55). The emphasis upon the paradox of 'Him whom the heavens cannot contain' being lodged in the Virgin's womb is, of course, entirely familiar in Nativity hymns; Donne borrows it, even to the usual word ('cloysterd'), for his repeated line in 'Annunciation' and 'Nativitie' in *La Corona*: 'Thou 'hast light in darke; and shutst in little roome,   *Immensity cloysterd in thy deare wombe.*'¹⁴ A Christ-mas responsory from 1 Kings viii. 27 is quoted in the *Speculum* with reference to both Virgin and Church: 'But will God indeed dwell on the earth? behold, the heaven and heaven of heavens cannot contain thee; how much less this house that I have builded?' It is, of course, the *taber-naculum* which holds the Eucharist; moreover, through cen-turies of use the verse 'Lord I am not worthy that thou shouldest come under my roof' (*sub tectum meum*) had be-come a metaphor for Holy Communion. When Herbert goes on from his I-am-too-little-for-thy-tabernacle image to 'when *thy* roof *my* soul hath hid' he is writing in paradox, doubly witty.

I do not take space to demonstrate it, but if any reader will re-read 'Temper, 1' he will see it widen and deepen when seen as a poem about the soul's possession or en-

¹⁴ Many of the witty paradoxes which form Donne's 'Annunciation' (ed. Grierson, i. 319) can be seen even in the single very well-known *Horae* Matins hymn *Quem terra pontus aethera* (printed in Fabricius, and, of course, frequently in *Horae*, missals, and breviaries, since it had several liturgical uses). The main paradox is that which Donne italicizes; the hymn marvels at how he who dwells in earth and sea and sky, who rules the three-fold fabric, is cloistered within Mary's frame; he whom sun, moon, and space serve is in the Virgin's body borne, the mother as in a casket encloses the great architect in whose fist is held all the world ('. . . claustrum Mariae, ventris sub arca clausus est', &c.). Donne writes: 'That All, which alwayes is All every where . . . yeelds himselfe to lye   In prison, in thy wombe . . . ere by the spheares time was created . . . Thou shutst in little roome . . . how he   Which fils all place, yet none holds him, doth lye.' Donne's conceit of 'Thy Makers maker, and thy Fathers mother' is so ubiquitous I have not space to cite Latin and vernacular hymns and lyrics, sequences, liturgical responses, a Petrarch madrigal set by Palestrina, &c. A good plain parallel is in the sequence *Hodiernae lux diei*: '. . . daughter the Sire to bear' (*Sarum Missal*, ii. 90; said daily much of the year; see also ii. 464, 'thou didst bring forth him that made thee').

closing of God; it elaborates as does 'Temper, II' (now seen to be closely connected) the immemorial metaphor of the human soul as God's dwelling or church, 'thy bower' where 'thy chair of grace' might be fixed. The many poems like 'Temper, I' dealing with Herbert's own states of spirit, which have so interested us moderns, are not to be separated off as showing some rebellious 'real' interest in himself that overcrowed his clerkly interest in the Church; they are poems about his state of mind *and* about *anima* as *ecclesia*, in his handling of the great traditional double conceit.

With the images of gilded *tabernaculum* and box-enclosed jewel we have insensibly moved on to another of Herbert's 'witty' images for the Virgin, in 'To all Angels and Saints' (p. 77):

> Thou art the holy mine, whence came the gold,
> The great restorative for all decay
>> In young and old;
> Thou art *the cabinet where the jewell lay*:
> Chiefly to thee would I my soul unfold. . . .

Gold as restorative, Christ as gold ('his head as the most fine gold', Song of Solomon v. 11), Christ as medicine and remedy for death, are, of course, conventions. And the preceding paragraphs show how traditional, how far from violent or surprising, and also how concentratedly meaningful is this figure of Mary—prime type of the Church of Christ—as jewel-enclosing cabinet. One of her oft-repeated 'names' is *sacrarium*. The feast of All Saints is the single one outside the great days of Christ's own mission (except Trinity) which Herbert chooses as subject of a poem in *The Temple*. This is no accident; the festival of the Church Triumphant is part of the theme of the book. That on that day he calls especially upon Mary is no accident but a remnant of the same liturgical tradition which Donne

echoes in his *Litanie*,[15] and it is equally no accident that
his crown-imagery echoes traditional liturgical martyr-
imagery and the Book of Revelation which was read upon
that day.

Another image in 'The Temper, I' (p. 55) which is a
favourite with Donne even more than with Herbert, and
which seems at first glance a peculiarly Metaphysical conceit, is that of man as God's music, his sinews or heart-
strings stretched like those of an instrument so that God's
music may be played upon him. It is witty and radical, but
obtrusively novel it would not be if we knew late medieval
symbolism. This has importance because more than one
poem which uses it would be easily damaged in tone by
the presence of attention-getting novelties. In this poem
Herbert says:

> Stretch or contract me, thy poore debter:
> This is but tuning of my breast,
>   To make the musick better.

Another appearance has more of the violence or shock
associated with Metaphysical wit; it shows, I believe, the
roots of the conceit:

> Awake, my lute, and struggle for thy part
>   With all thy art.
> The crosse taught all wood to resound his name,
>   Who bore the same.

---

[15] The relation to All Saints' Day liturgy is shown by Donne's inclusion of
the *Doctores* in his list of persons invoked, otherwise the conventional medieval
and Catholic (not Anglican) list. I had conjectured that the Donne who had
his *Hymn* set to music and sung by the St. Paul's choristers ('O the power of
Church-music': Walton quotes him as saying) was perhaps especially struck by
the inclusion of the *Doctores* in the motets for All Saints' Day; e.g. Gabrieli's
Angeli archangeli, Palestrina's *Salvator mundi* (Leipzig ed. v. 23). Most pertinent
of all is the appearance of the *Doctores* in the litany for this day, as my friend
Miss H. Gardner noticed and will point out in her forthcoming edition of the
Divine Poems.

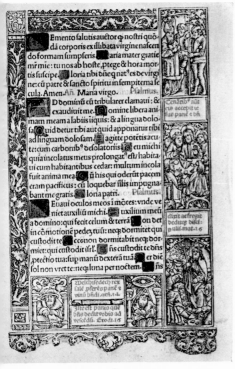

a

b

X *a. Speculum hum. salv.*, B.Mus. MS.
Harl. 2838, f. 15ʳ, xv c.: Naaman,
Ark over Jordan

X *b. Horae*, 1513 (Kerver): Melchisedec, L. Supper, Manna

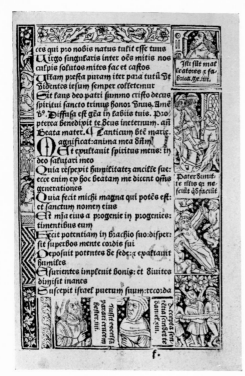

XI *a. Speculum hum. salv.*, B. M
MS. Harl. 2838, f. 25ᵛ, xv c.: Ch
nailed, Invention of music

XI *b. Horae*, 1488/9 (Dupré): Inv
tion of music, Christ nailed, Isa
sawn

His stretched sinews taught all strings, what key
Is best to celebrate this most high day.

Consort both heart and lute, and twist a song . . .

This is 'Easter' (p. 41). It quotes directly from the Easter
proper psalm, 57 ('awake, lute and harp: I myself will
awake right early'). From the semi-punning *sursum corda* of
its first line ('Rise heart; thy Lord is risen') to its close with
the hymn-like second part it proclaims itself one of that
semi-liturgical lyrical genre to which scores of medieval
poems belong. With all its 'sweets' brought for tribute early
on the spring morning of the great Day, the whole poem is
a *Salve festa dies* like that famous Easter processional of
Venantius Fortunatus.

The basic 'concept' of the 'conceit' quoted is the crucified
Christ as a lyre, Love as music; and just so in the *Speculum
humanae salvationis* 'Christ was stendid [extended] on the
crosse/ als in ane harpe ere the stringes'. 'O lord how this
faire harpe [*cithara*]/gaf a swete melody!' says the text,
accompanying the pictures of the Crucifixion and of
David's dance before the Ark of the Testament, prefiguring
Christ by his harping. Another set (in *Horae* and *Biblia Pauperum* also; see Plate XI *a, b*) pictures Tubalcain and Jubal,
finders of the arts of ironwork and of music, the first with
his hammer whose sounds set the second to invent or find
music; they are a type of the hammering of Christ on to
the Cross with nails, and the melody He found was that
speech celebrated as the quintessence of Love, 'Father for-
give them for they know not what they do'. This last connexion is found also in Ludolphe de Saxe's popular *Vita
Christi*, ii, ch. 63. A discourse upon Love in the *Speculum*
emphasizes that basic metaphorical identification of *caritas*
with music, or harmony, which gives life to other music-
images in Herbert. The same ancient metaphor clarifies

Donne's lines on the many-membered world as the 'Organ'
and on Elizabeth Drury as a type of both harmony and
love:

> But those fine spirits which do tune, and set
> This Organ, are those peeces which beget
> Wonder and love; and these were shee. . . .

> (Grierson, i. 246.)

Lord Harrington's fair soul was 'harmony', 'as all soules
bee', and now after his death it bears a part 'in Gods great
organ, this whole Spheare' (i. 271). A long and more complex use of the conceit of the great organ of the universe,
tuned by Christ, appears in Donne's verses on Philip and
Mary Sidney's translation of the Psalms: 'The Organist is
hee   Who hath tun'd God and Man, the Organ we';
brother and sister are made by God 'The Organ, where
thou art the Harmony' (i. 348-9).

The whole conceit is simply a specifically musical form,
in more Christian phrasing, of the great metaphor which
we are so familiar with (in Spenser and other poets) in
neo-Platonic or cosmological phrasing, i.e. Love as concord and harmony between dissimilars. The overtones in
Herbert's uses of the image are always Christian and sometimes churchly. The connexion with Christ as Love, the
new Law, is clearest in 'Aaron' (p. 174): 'I have . . .
Another musick, making live not dead,   Without whom
I could have no rest', 'Christ is . . . My onely musick',
'My doctrine tun'd by Christ'. I do not trouble to cite a
close medieval parallel in *La Lumière as Lais*, and I doubt
if Herbert ever saw it. What we can only call 'tradition'
accounts for the persistent appearance of these old similitudes; see another form of it in 'Providence': 'all must
appeare,   And be dispos'd, and dress'd, and tun'd by
thee,   Who sweetly temper'st all. If we could heare

Thy skill and art, what musick would it be!' (p. 118). Or see 'Deniall' (p. 79): 'my soul lay . . . Untun'd, un-strung: . . . O cheer and tune my heartlesse breast, Deferre no time.' This is probably an Advent poem, with its italicized *veni veni* like the Seven Great Oes of Advent, and its metrical device by which only God's *coming* to the human heart will 'mend the ryme' (literally providing the first final rhyme in any stanza). 'Christmas', which follows, plays upon and finally repeats the music conceit: 'His beams shall cheer my breast, and both so twine, Till ev'n his beams sing, and my musick shine' (p. 80).

One element more in the whole motif may be typified by Donne's best-known use of it:

> Since I am comming to that Holy roome,
>   Where, with thy Quire of Saints for evermore,
> I shall be made thy Musique; As I come
>   I tune the Instrument here at the dore,
>   And what I must doe then, thinke here before.

('Hymne to God, in my sicknesse', i. 368.)

This is a context and use popularized through the often-printed 'Stimulus amoris' attributed variously to Anselm and Bernard, where a closing description of the joys of the saints in the heavenly Jerusalem tells how 'those glorious and flamie Organs [*organa*] doe incessantly sing Hymnes' (R. B.'s translation, 1614; see below, n. 27 and text). In Herbert's 'Dooms-day', the Lord will raise his 'broken consort' (pun), all the dead now become dust which 'no musick feels, But thy trumpet' (p. 186).

Though prophets (and preachers) are traditionally the Church's *bells*, or *trumpets*, I do not think Donne's pro-phets as the 'Churches Organs' primarily a use of this music conceit, but rather a way of stating the tradition of typology—the prophets sounded 'That harmony, which

made of two   One law, and did unite, but not con-
found'.[16] A critic citing relations with emblems should not
conclude that Donne was 'anxious to enrich his imagery
by *novel* . . . metaphors'—the 'novelty' is in our own
minds, perhaps also the anxiety for it. Of course, we could
not begin to count the number of times we meet choirs of
apostles, prophets as sweet-sounding bells, the whole *dulci-
sona organa omnium sanctorum* in liturgy and treatise; it is perhaps worth while to cite two. The martyrs peculiarly are
made God's music. The sequence for the Common of a
Martyr, *Organicis canamus*, in the Sarum Use (which Donne
at least certainly knew) begins: In the saints, 'as though in
instruments of music, faith doth with her own finger touch
the strings . . .', discoursing high of virtues excellent, laying
her hand on each string and composing their harmonious
symphony (*Sarum Missal*, ii. 13). And a sequence of Adam
of St. Victor's, used on St. Lawrence's day, has a verse
Sicut chorda musicorum in which (as in Herbert and in the
Speculum) the martyrs give forth the best tone when their
sinews are made tense by the torments they suffer for Christ.[17]

Thus, although this conceit is not, like some others I
treat, a universally used and deep-reaching symbol kindling
whole trains of underground meanings, it is nevertheless
surely clear that when Donne and Herbert use it they are not
exercising some peculiarly seventeenth-century form of wit
by which we are to define their difference from earlier poets.

[16] 'Litanie', i. 340; the figure is more like that in 'harmony of the gospels' and
is not the same image as that to which J. Lederer tries to relate it in 'John Donne
and the Emblematic Practice', *RES*, xxii (1946), p. 193, quoting very late
(1653) remnants in emblem literature of the old conceits; some of them are more
pertinent, however, than this one.

[17] This sequence, *Prunis datum admiremur*, was printed in Clichtoveus (see
Note on accessibility of such materials, at the end of the book), but it was not
in the Sarum Use. This 'well-tempered' element in the figure is I suppose
combined in Herbert's title 'The Temper' with a hint of the tempering of steel
and with the meaning 'restraint within due limits'.

Indeed nothing is more common in medieval religious allegorical poetry—of which some is good and some bad, as is usual in human affairs—than the 'blend of wit and tenderness' which J. B. Leishman remarks upon in connexion with another Herbert image. This is natural enough; such blends are the whole point of the figure *allegoria*. 'Dulnesse' (p. 115), which is a poem contrasting sacred and profane love and asking Christ for 'quicknesse, that I may . . .praise' Him, has these two stanzas:

> The wanton lover in a curious strain
> Can praise his fairest fair;
> And with quaint metaphors her curled hair
> Curl o're again.

> Thou art my lovelinesse, my life, my light,
> Beautie alone to me:
> Thy bloudy death and undeserv'd, makes thee
> Pure red and white.

Leishman comments: 'even that conceit about red and white, which many would find offensive, seems to me, I must admit, entirely in keeping with the whole tone of the poem, and not at all extravagant' (see Hutchinson's notes). Those who find this offensive must needs be frequently offended if they read much poetry and prose written on this subject; that cannot be extravagant which walks within the conventional bounds. The convention doubtless sprang from the words applied to Christ as the soul's lover, 'My beloved is white and ruddy' (Song of Solomon, v. 10; the antiphon *Dilectus meus*, and motet *Adjuro vos filiae*, e.g. Palestrina, iv. 19); no one was unaware of the secular uses of the phrase. The many commentaries and references relate the *candidus* to His divinity, the *rubicundus* to His Passion, or contrast the spotless loveliness of His birth and life to the bloody martyrdom of His unjust death. As in Herbert, *all beauty* and *all love* are comprehended in the two symbolic epithets. The *white* vestment and the *red* are allegorically written of in the *Speculum humanae salvationis* (ch. 30, 20); the 'pourpre vermeille' robe of the Flagellation is red with the *blood* shed for love, and the white robe in which Christ was mocked by Herod secretly and ironically showed his *innocence.* 'Thy *bloudy* death and *undeserv'd*, makes thee Pure *red* and *white*', says Herbert, with the same simultaneous conveying of concept and physically seen image, the same lighting up of several facets of meaning at once, which is the usual operation of symbolic figures. Hence the blending of wit with feeling, of ratiocination with passion, which characterizes all good poetry using *allegoria*, the extremest form of metaphor. We do not always catch the wit unless we share knowledge possessed by our predecessors, nor the passion unless we share their conceptions of what is important.

The epithets of white and red early displaced other possible sensuously descriptive adjectives in lyrics of Christ crucified, partly because of a very famous passage in the Meditations ascribed to St. Augustine: '*Candet* nudatum pectus. *Rubet* cruentum latus . . .'; lyrics adapting the actual passage generally begin 'White was his naked breast and red of blood his side'. Other lyrics of the same general type begin '*Look*, man . . .', or '*Look*, at thy lord', sometimes incorporating the *candet . . . rubet* passage, and translating another popular Latin meditation beginning '*Respice* in faciem Christi'. This passage too had wide currency, inserted in popular books like Ludolphus's *Vita Christi* and Richard Rolle's *Incendium Amoris*, and it seems almost inevitable that Herbert's poem should end 'that . . . I may but look towards thee: *Look* onely' (his italics). It was also conventional for Complaints of Christ on the Cross to begin, '*Homo, vide* quid pro te patior'. Although we cannot tell, and do not care, what form Herbert knew of the mingled *candet . . . rubet* and *respice* motifs, it is proper when our concern is with the naturalness as compared with the extravagancy of his language to recognize that such long-traditional usage must have made it doubly natural to him.[18] Equally to be expected in a 'Christ my leman' poem are the very choice of a Crucifixion image and the emphasis upon his own earthy 'dulnesse'.

All the images we have been considering in the last dozen pages have been witty, radical, and apt—and thoroughly conventional. This combination may seem no happy dis-covery to us, accustomed to a late-Romantic association between the witty and the audaciously unconventional, and to praises of the first based on interest in the second. I think that nothing but good, for the poems, comes of disrupting this association and of foregoing these praises, founded as both are on rather superficial notions of individuality and originality. Poems meant to be quietly moving will be differently read from poems meant to startle. They may gain in depth of meaning. My final instances of witty conven-tional images belong together in a definable group—from the poems on the church as a building with its parts, its adjuncts, its ornaments, and its priest. They have brought on Herbert more than one charge (sometimes even thought of as praise) of novel quaintness and engagingly childish *naïveté*; of late they have rather been seen as 'Metaphysi-cally' clever, chiefly pleasurable for their capacity to surprise through dissonant and unexpected combinations.

---

[18] The Aug. meditation is referred to above, e.g. Part I, n. 28; a Latin text is conveniently printed in *Patr. Lat.* 40: 906. See C. Brown, *Religious Lyrics of the xivth Century*, notes to no. 1 and 2. The *respice* passage comes originally from Ps. 84. 9. Commentaries and glosses on the Song of Sol. or 'expositions' like Honorius's, Alanus's, &c., can be consulted without more definite references. For a relating of the *white* and *red* to Christ's *Body* and *Blood*, the *bread* and *wine*, and to Christ the *granum frumenti* white within and red without, dying to live again, see Hugh of St. Victor's *Speculum ecclesiae*, *Patr. Lat.* 177: 363.

I have remarked that Herbert follows a tradition of long standing in many arts in centring his book around Ecclesia and the New Dispensation of heavenly love. The very notion of a group of poems about the physical aspects of the Church is conventional; more than one medieval *Speculum ecclesiae* reprinted in the Renaissance allegorizes as Herbert does altar, windows, church floor, music, antiphons, celebrants and their vestments, and goes on to treat of the various hours (see Herbert's 'Mattens', 'Even-song', a group on the Holy Communion) and then of the Church year with its various feasts. A glance at Herbert's table of contents will show how many of his poems are subsumed under the series Advent, Nativity, Ash Wednesday and Lent, Holy Week, Easter, Ascension, Whitsun, and some special days like Trinity Sunday and All Saints; also, many more of the poems are Lenten or Holy Week poems than we have recognized. Durandus's *Rationale* is the most common and frequently printed such treatise.[19] But his organization, and allegorical interpretations such as I shall mention, are commonplaces, many of them to be found e.g. in Hugh of St. Victor, in Joannes Belethus, or in the *Gemma animae* of Honorius Augustodunensis. All were reprinted in the sixteenth and seventeenth centuries and some (especially the last) got into the current anthologies of liturgical treatises.

In Durandus's *Rationale* the altar is the heart (Herbert's 'Altar', p. 26, is 'Made of a heart, and cemented with teares'); the church-floor is *humilitas cordis* (in Herbert, p. 66,

[19] Very frequent in manuscript, and often reprinted. In an old library like Bodley one may count twenty-five editions between the 1470's and 1614. Vérard printed a French translation in 1503. Only Book I (which does, however, include the church and its parts) is translated in J. M. Neale and B. Webb, *Symbolism of Churches and Church Ornaments*, London, 1906, but a French translation by Charles Barthélemy, Paris, 1854, is complete. For the other similar treatises next mentioned (texts here cited from *Patr. Lat.*) see the Note at the end of the book, on accessibility of such materials.

the black squares of the chequered floor are Humility, the speckled ones Patience; God is blest who 'Could build so strong in a weak heart'). The poor in spirit are the pavement of the spiritual Church in Belethus's *Rationale* (ch. 103) because of their humility. Durandus's windows are *dicta sanctorum*; or the glass of the windows is the Holy Scriptures, which transmit to the Church (the hearts of the faithful) the light of the true Sun. In Herbert's 'The Windows', p. 67, the preacher himself is both window and glass, transmitting the doctrine of the Eternal Word to the faithful, and, if he lives a Christ-like life, 'annealing in glasse' God's story even more winningly and gloriously, because thus in colours rather than 'watrish, bleak, & thin'. Honorius, writing 'Of the windows of the church' in the *Gemma animae*, makes them represent the *doctors* of the church, who transmit the light of true doctrine, and the glass is *mens doctorum*. And in the same author's well-known *Elucidarium* a chapter 'De Ecclesiae ministris' makes these *fenestrae in domo Domini*, while the very question Herbert takes up—of the preacher who has merely doctrine compared with him who also lives a God-like life—is discussed in several sentences, though new images are introduced instead of Herbert's extension of the common image to make his preacher a stained-glass historiated window.[20]

This is typical of Herbert's writing; using a traditional central invention or imaginative similitude, he bores down within it to discover new veins of meaning. The method and the nature of the witty parallels, and the simultaneous presentation of the physical church and the temple built in the heart as one and the same thing, are traditional.

The allegorizing of the priest's vestments, using the

[20] For Honorius see *Patr. Lat.* 172, cols. 1148, 586. On the *bells* image I next discuss see Honorius, 172: 588 (also the *vessels*), and Hugh of St. Victor's *Speculum ecclesiae, Patr. Lat.* 177: 336; chapters on vestments follow shortly in both.

description of Aaron's clothing in Exod. xxviii but turning
all into figures for the qualities and powers which the priest
of God should 'wear', is another case in point. Herbert em-
ploys details from this cluster of traditional images several
times, and constructs one beautiful poem, 'Aaron' (p. 174),
with this allegorical convention as the warp, weaving into
it another inherited image of man as Christ's music.
'Aaron' begins:

> Holinesse on the head,
> Light and perfections on the breast,
> Harmonious bells below, raising the dead
> To leade them unto life and rest:
> Thus are true Aarons drest.

But he himself, alas, wears on his forehead no Aaron's
lamina inscribed HOLINESS TO THE LORD, there is rather
'*Profanenesse* in *my* head'; in his breast only '*darknesse*' and
'*defects*', instead of the *light* of doctrine and *perfection* of truth
(Vulgate: *Doctrinam et Veritatem*; King J.: Urim and
Thummim). The bells on the garment hem, which were
to sound as Aaron moved 'that he die not', and by which
he, Herbert, should call others to life and rest, are become
a mere noise of passions, proclaiming him dead to his
priesthood—'Poore priest thus am I drest'. So far only the
Old Testament symbolism. But then he bethinks himself
that he has 'another head . . . another heart and breast'—
Christ, his head, his new breast-plate of judgement, in
whom he is 'new drest', Christ his music (his 'doctrine
tun'd by Christ'), who lives in him to be sounded out to
others. So! the bells can ring, the people gather, 'Come
people; Aaron's drest'.

The most popular of these traditional allegorical images
is that of the bells as the preacher, 'who convokes the people
to the church', whose words sound out the Gospel to the

ends of the earth. Honorius explains it (*De campanis*), so do Belethus, and Durandus commenting on the silence of Tenebrae, and Hugh of St. Victor in his *Speculum ecclesiae*. It got into the tidily indexed and frequently printed handbooks of *Figurae Bibliorum*; see that of Antony de Rampegollis (s.v. *sacerdos*; I use Cologne, 1609). Rabanus' *Allegoriae* has it under *tintinnabula*. The ubiquitous Peter Comestor (widely popular in French as the *Bible historiale*) comments on those priests whose care for their flocks is shown in their sounding of their bells, 'non debent esse muti sacerdotes' (ch. 64, Exod.). This last element in the motif will crop up in any odd place, as in a sermon, *Christs Suite to his Church*, preached by Thomas Myriell at Paul's Cross in 1613, citing Aaron's bells and remarking that a preacher dieth if there be no preaching in his mouth.[21] We cannot be surprised that it should thus crop up, since Gregory has it in both *Pastoral Care* and *Epistles* (ii, ch. 4; Ep. 25); and it has left its trace on Herbert's first stanza in his substitution of the preacher's duty to lead his people to life and rest through the sounding of his bells, for the Old Testament notion of Aaron's bells sounding 'that he not die'.

Herbert uses 'great Aarons bell' again as an image for the priest sounding forth God's presence in 'Decay' (p. 99). This poem's theme is related to that of 'Aaron' as the other side of the medal, for it treats of God's withdrawal from open accessibility into 'some one corner of a feeble heart',

---

[21] This book is a typical illustration of the period's familiarity with typology. With citations to the fathers in the margin, it has many of Herbert's and Donne's images: the Sidewounding when the Church was born out of Christ's side, paralleled with the creation of Eve; Moses striking the rock and the stream from Christ's side; Christ our Samson bearing away the gates; His wounds to hide in (holes in the rock); various forms of the Song of Sol. spouse conceit, including Christ's choosing of the ugly black one, cleansing and decking and rescuing her, and Christ's Church as the dove (see all these in Donne's sonnet xviii); bees as the hieroglyph of chastity (cf. Herbert, p. 118); Christ the Ram.

and of Love thus closeted up 'as in an urn' (the *tabernaculum* image), but in a faulty one, where it is crowded by Sin and Satan. God's Church as Love in the Heart did not always seem possible of success to Herbert, and here he thinks of Love (Christ, of course) as forced out of its too 'pinched and straitened' corner some time to return 'And calling JUSTICE, all things burn'.

Although Aaron's bells are the most charming and most popular of these priesthood–images, the allegorizing of the 'breastplate of judgment' from Exodus as *Christ's* doctrine and His truth, and the whole notion of the typological parallel, underlie Herbert's invention in 'Aaron'. His use of the single set of five rhyme–words through his develop– ment in the five stanzas is no trick, but merely another facet of that symbolizing of the sublime unity of a twofold revela– tion which he presents to us in poem after poem. Certain related images dependent on biblical suggestion, and used by Herbert, had also been emphasized by traditional expan– sion or interpretation. For example, in 'The Priesthood' (p. 160): 'exchanging my lay–sword   For that of th'holy Word' (in Durandus, the tongue of the preacher is his sword; cf., of course, Eph. vi and the 'mouth like a sharp sword' of Isa. xlix. 2); or the commonplace 'holy men of God' as 'vessels' (cf. Honorius: bells have a vessel–like form, 'quia predicatores vasa Spiritus sancti appellantur'). Recalling the symbolism of the ark: *tabernaculum*: Ecclesia, we realize that it is not only some chance remembrance of a Bible verse that makes him say in the same poem, 'I dare not, I, put forth my hand   To hold the Ark, although it seem to shake   Through th'old sinnes and new doc– trines of our land'. 'Thy floting Ark' in 'Affliction, v' (p. 97) has reference throughout the poem to another con– ventional parallel—of the Church with Noah's ark, safe against the tossing seas of this world.

One other very common image for the preacher may or may not be responsible for Herbert's fondness for the image of 'wings' in connexion with his own need for inspiration. According to the *Glossa ordinaria* the silver wings of the dove (in Ps. 68) are the preachers who carry aloft the glory of the Church; according to Augustine (Enarr. on that Psalm) the Church is borne up, as on wings, by the preaching of the faithful; the wings are silvered because with divine sayings the Church has been instructed, and golden with the love shed abroad by the Holy Spirit. This is used, for example, by Myriell in the sermon referred to just above; preachers bear up the whole body of the Church, let them preach diligently, says he, 'For a dumbe Minister is as a clipt wing' which lets the body fall (pp. 62–63). Herbert prays 'I go to Church; help me to wings' in 'Praise, 1' (p. 61); he wishes that he may 'imp my wing on thine' in his wing-shaped poem, 'Easter-wings' (p. 43). I mention only these two because the poems they come from are surprisingly more meaningful if read as the utterances of Herbert not only as 'any Christian' but consciously in his character as priest and preacher. There is assuredly a connexion between the conventional image and the first two lines of 'Whitsunday' (p. 59), which is a poem speci-fically about the spreading of the gospel through the preachers of the word:

> Listen sweet Dove unto my song,
> And spread thy golden wings in me. . . .

The wings are golden because of the remainder of the verse in this same Ps. 68, a Whitsun proper psalm for centuries in Sarum Use (reinstated for that feast, 1662 BCP), and in the Anglican Church during Herbert's ministry used for the nearby feast of the Ascension.[22]

[22] 'Though ye have lien among the pots, yet shall ye be as the wings of a dove: that is covered with silver wings, and her feathers like gold.' It is entirely usual

I think it is clear against the background of the last few pages that it is a falsification for us to think of Herbert's images about the Church's building, contents, and priest as if they were original and ingenious in the usual sense. These are in the same case as the other witty, homely, sup-posedly peculiarly Metaphysical images—the conceits about music, Mary, the red and white Christ; when we approach them innocent of their long use, traditional overtones, and serious fitness deriving from long-familiar connexions, we not only outright lose shades of meaning but we destroy the delicacy and decorous justness of the tone. The tone of a poem is our way to know what it means, what it is as a formal reality in its own right. I would call attention to the fact that often what we require is plain ordinary in-formation, for that is what time and history have done us out of. In the approach to poems, as in the approach to reality in any other form, we have a right to only a limited amount of ignorance, or we shall quite simply not under-stand what we see. It is perfectly possible to claim that Herbert's poems are not worth the labour of understanding them, and I have been at pains to meet that objection. This is very different from the claim that understanding is not valuably or reliably advanced by information directly bear-ing on consciously intended meaning. Not until modern times has such a position been considered tenable by any serious criticism; it is now widely held.

§ 3. *Explanation*

The images so far treated have all been cases in which a knowledge of earlier symbolic uses of truly witty conceits

to find double, even triple, symbolism (the Dove is the Holy Spirit, of course, and often Ecclesia, as in Donne's sonnet xviii). Herbert owned 'Augustines workes'; see his Will in Hutchinson, p. 382.

changes our reaction from one of shock, or admiration of adroit contrivance, into a quieter response that notices instead the deeper meanings of whole poems and the relation of single images to large themes, or at least notices fitness rather than baroque violence. Many times such knowledge has a simpler but equally satisfactory result: it simply *explains* what would otherwise look like an odd by-way of thought, an eccentric or obscure relationship.

A case of seeming eccentricity is the poem 'Sunday' (p. 75), especially for the oddity of the 'unhinging of Sunday' image, with its dragging in of Samson. But there is no peculiarity in Herbert's thought here as he explains and makes a metaphor out of the substitution of Christian Sunday for Hebrew Seventh Day. All follows quite fitly from 'This day my Saviour rose', and Samson is next to Jonah the most familiar of all Easter-season types.

> The rest of our Creation
> Our great Redeemer did remove
> With the same shake, which at his passion
> Did th'earth and all things with it move.
> As Sampson bore the doores away,
> Christs hands, though nail'd, wrought our salvation,
> And did unhinge that day.

Here I am certain that it is iconographical convention which bound author and readers together in common understanding of an image. It would be quite impossible to count the number of Samsons one can meet with— always the same figure with the flat, plank-like gates of Gaza on his shoulder (plainly showing their hinges), always stepping vigorously up his hill, and always shown in conjunction with Christ risen from His tomb. The *Biblia Pauperum*, stained glass accompanied by verses as at St. Albans and Canterbury, the margins of a multitude of *Horae* or of 'Queen Elizabeth's Prayerbook', all combined to give the

pictured parallel figures extreme currency and familiarity
(see Plates XII *a*, *b*, *c*, XIII *a*). The *Speculum humanae salvationis* adds to its pictures a careful explanation of the fact
that just as Samson bore away the gates in the middle of
the night, so Christ waited from Friday until just after midnight Sunday morning before delivering the captives of
hell. The *Speculum* dwells also on the earth-trembling; the
risen Christ is the Judge; *Terra tremuit* is the offertorium for
Easter Sunday, and Herbert's other use of the Samson
image is in his *Terrae-motus* (p. 408). As usual there are
plenteous other more learned appearances of the parallel
image: in the *Glossa ordinaria*; in handbooks like Antony
de Rampegollis's *Figurae Bibliorum* (s.v. *De resurr.*); the very
well-known Easter sequence by Adam of St. Victor, *Zyma
vetus expurgetur*, introduces this among its types ('Lex est
umbra futurorum . . . Samson Gazę seras pandit   et
asportans portas scandit   montis supercilium').

I should mention before leaving the poem 'Sunday' that
if it seems to us a little strange of Herbert to write a poem
at all on this subject, and to think of the Sundays of the
Church year as 'bracelets to adorn the wife   Of the
eternal glorious King', it probably did not seem so to those
familiar with a whole set of verses on the days of the week,
appearing in the common Primers. 'I am Sunday honour-
able   *The heed* of all the weke dayes', begins one;[23] Herbert
says, 'The other dayes and thou   Make up one man;
whose *face* thou art,   Knocking at heaven with *thy brow*'.
And the Sarum Missal sees heaven figured in Sunday.
Explaining why mass is celebrated on Saturdays for the
Virgin, 'the gate of heaven', it says that Saturday is a door
and entrance to Sunday; being in Our Lady's grace on Saturdays we are at least 'in the door of paradise', for Sunday

[23] This happens to be from the Sarum Primer STC 15994. For the Sarum
Missal references see Warren's translation, ii. 74.

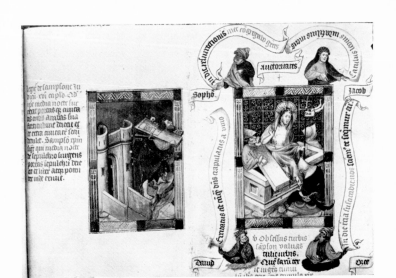

XII a. *Mirouer de redempcion*, 1493: Resurr., Samson

XII c. *Horae*, 1497 (Kerver): Samson, Resurr.,
Jonah

XII b. *Biblia Pauperum*, B.Mus. MS. King's 5, f. 20ʳ: Samson, Resurr.

XIII *a*. Enamelled panels, xii c., B.Mus.: Naaman.   Samson.

XIII *b*. *Biblia Pauperum*, B.Mus. MS. King's 5, f. 18ʳ, *c*. 1400:
Eve's creation, Side-wound

Unsers herren nadtmal Matheus. rrvi
Marcus am· riiij· Lucas am· rrij· Johan-
nes am· riij· Das· rrvi·capitel·

¶ Dem fünfzehenden capitel hôt
tem zeit von cristus ere nün füllen
wir hôrê von sinem nachtmal vñ
von der heiligen gemeinsamkeit sines lieb
nams· Do die spt kam daz cristus wolte
die matter spten zu wrare er zu rore das
er wolte uff secze die heiligen gemeinsam
keit des sacramentes· das ist sines heiligen
lidnamen zu einre ewigen gedenknüss·
vñ das er vns sine süsse mynne erzeygte
So wolte er sich selber vns zu einre spisse
geben·❖·

❡ Diß heilige sacramente was die
der bezeichent· Das hymmel brot
das die noch den iuden in der wüs
ste gegeben wart von dem hymmele· uñ
⟨…⟩

ten hymmel vnd hies doch hymmelbrot ·
wen es warr geschaffen ton zoren in des
lüffte oder in des lüffes hymmel· ¶ Aber
cristus vnser behalter der ist das wore le
bendige brot das von des hymmel her ab
ist kumen vnd vns vnser spiß zorten· Got
gap zm iuden die bezeichunge des zoren
brotes· Aber vns har er geben mit die be
zachungs· wen er har vns geben die zoren
het des wors brotes· Das hymmelbrot
hat die nature das es by der sunnen sdyn
zerschmelze· vnd by dem füre hert wart
Also wergar vnd schmilzget das zoren hy
melbrot in den irdyigen hertzen· Aber in
de füren hertze werdmerkte es nit· Das
hymmelbrot schmackte einem iegidlich⟨…⟩

men soul uff gelesen so sü hon komen
so hatt· doch regidicher fin meß soul· Also
ist es auch der das sacramente empfohet
das wore hymmelbrot der vil hoffigen
müsse· der het doch nicht me zoren der nu
wont eine müsse· Vnd der der zu nymmet
ein clein früdlin von der hoffigem der hat
nit mynre zoren der der ein gantze oder etz
zre menige hymmet

Die iuden offent das osterlamp
bi am· riij·capitel ·❖·

louten· Vnd füllent auch uffrecht sten in
gütem leben das sü han angefangen· vñ
füllent sich mit zorter in das recht legt· vf
fer dem sü erstant· sine· Sü offent das lap
mit zorter laudet die was bitter· vñ zort
füllent den hymmlidem lidnam nützgen mit
bitterer ru zoen· Eve das lamp offent die
solten gefdolher fin· vnd by sü füllen reg
tent zegedent heilige zegieres· Also süllet
die die das sacramente empfohent die füll
lent gefdolher fin vnd füllent sich pütre ez·
ir begirte mit keiner vnreinikeit bemolset
zore· Das osterlamp was gebôtt mit
füre vnd mit wasser gesotten· Also sol
ter der das sacramente nüsset von liechte fü
rig fin des es zoruôichen müsse·

❡ Melchisedech brachte Abraham brot
vnd zoin·

Als adam bel vnsers herren teus
ouch bie vor zorgedent by dem
osterlambe· das die iuden spulize
ten zü essen am karnosdag vor dem kar
fridage· Das osterlamp getett got zm iu
den zü dem erst zü essen vnd zorôte sü bo
mit lôsen vß dem land egipten· ¶ Also fa
ste ouch cristus das sacrament vff·tor er
vns zorôte erlôsen von des tüfels gewalt·
Do die iuden das osterlamp offent to zoo
⟨…⟩

❡ Cristus farzte das sacramêt of vn
ter der form brotes vnd zoines·
Das was hie vor betzachent by
⟨…⟩

XIV. *Spiegel mensch. Behalt.*, 1476: Last Supper, Manna, Lamb, Melchisedec

XV. *Biblia Pauperum*, block-book, B.Mus.: Melchisedec, L. Supper, Manna symbolizes eternal life. This kind of double significance for the day puts the firmness of a thought under Herbert's 'Sun day... the next worlds bud,   Th'indorsement of supreme delight [i.e. of the final felicity],   Writ by a friend, and with his bloud'; 'On Sunday heavens gate stands ope'.

One of Herbert's most characteristic poems is 'Peace' (p. 124). I trust to the reader's familiarity with its allegorical narrative, the story of the search here and there through the world, of the meeting with the 'rev'rend good old man' who told the seeker how

> There was a Prince of old
> At Salem dwelt, who liv'd with good increase
> Of flock and fold.
>
> He sweetly liv'd; yet sweetnesse did not save
> His life from foes.
> But after death out of his grave
> There sprang twelve stalks of wheat:
> Which many wondring at, got some of those
> To plant and set. . . .
>
> Take of this grain, which in my garden grows, . . .
> Make bread of it. . . .

As Hutchinson says in his notes, Vaughan realized that Herbert wrote of Christ, for Melchisedec, 'King of Salem, which is, King of peace' (Heb. vii. 2), prefigured Christ. Not only is this true, but the centuries which had made this one of the firmest of all symbolic conventions had so ecclesiasticized it that none could be more suited to Her bert's unifying theme. Few could be unaware that Mel chisedec the Priest King prefigured Christ in his character as the Eucharist; Melchisedec's action in giving bread and wine to Abraham is the Old Testament type of Christ's feeding of His Church, and Christ is the God who nourishes, the Priest who officiates, the King, and the sacrifice (the Body, Bread, spiritual food) which is eaten. This is a Holy Communion poem, but it is also a poem of the apostles' mission, and of *corpus* Christi as the Bread but simultaneously as that 'mystical Body' of Christ of whom men may become 'very members incorporate'.

In both the *Biblia Pauperum* and the *Speculum*, the *Coena domini* (the conventional picturing of the Lord's Supper with the disciples) is flanked by a picture of Melchisedec as priest (bishop) with chalice ministering to Abraham (a knight, and often kneeling), and by a picture of the manna —the first *panis angelicus*, type of Christ—dropping from heaven like little round coins upon the Chosen People (see Plates XIV, XV, X *b*, IV, and above, Part I, n. 23, 24 and text). No iconographical symbol is more constant than this one—from the time of Abbot Suger at St. Denis, at Chartres, at Reims, at Amiens, at Peterborough, in illu-minated psalters, down to the triple marginal vignettes of uncountable *Horae* and of the Books of Christian Prayers that copied them. Rhyming verses often accompanied the appearances in stained glass, as at St. Albans, and at Canterbury (still intact in Herbert's time). *Melchisedek rex Salem*, proclaims the side-text in various *Horae* of Sarum Use,[24] picturing also, of course, the *Coena* and Manna, as

[24] e.g. in several from Kerver's press, whence issued some of the most delicate and lovely *Horae*; STC 15885, illustrated in Plate V *b* from the Folger copy, is one of the earliest. The chief names in connexion with *Horae* showing the typological series are Kerver (also for Ricard, for Bretton), Pigouchet, S. Vostre, de Marnef, Vérard, Dupré. The last-named is of especial importance, for he prints a forty-nine-item 'repertoire' of the series of O.T. types each 'signifians une vraye histoire du nouveau', and including the biblical references, connexions which were often, of course, of liturgical origin. See Brit. Mus. copy, IA 39821 sgs. [ ] 2 verso to 4 verso. The press of J. Daye began the series of 'Queen Elizabeth's Prayerbooks'; see STC 6428 ff. For the *Hours*, STC listings do not cover the matter, as books not only of Sarum but of Roman, Rouen, Paris, and other Uses also circulated. I am sure that we ought to remember oftener, for all questions touching artistic conventions, that men did not wait for the century of Morgan, Huntington, Harmsworth *et al.* to look at beautiful books. As I once overheard at a lecture wherein occurred that old unhappy far-off thing about

usual. The text of the *Speculum* discusses various aspects of the parallel—kingship, priesthood; and Christ as *rex pacificus*, &c., is a liturgical commonplace in feasts of the relevant seasons. The epistle to the Hebrews, which repeatedly relates Christ and Melchisedec, lacks, of course, the churchly symbolism and the extreme vividness of the visual convention; Herbert read out Hebrews year after year at the Evensongs of the Lenten and Paschal season.

I suppose that without instruction we would figure out Herbert's twelve stalks of wheat as the twelve apostles, and the 'strange prospering' as the establishment of the Church among the Gentiles. But as with the Prince of Salem it seems important to recognize the familiarity and uneccentric character of the grain-figure for Christ. The metaphor of Christ as the corn of wheat that must fall into the ground and die in order to bring forth fruit arises from His own words in John xii. 24. But medieval commentaries, liturgical treatises, and homilies, the *Glossa ordinaria* quoting Augustine, &c., had made conventional the assumption that this *granum frumenti* is the Bread with which the Church nourishes man, also the Church itself as the Body of Christ. In iconography also the connexion with the apostles' mission appears; the (12) prophets bring the grain, St. Paul turns the mill that makes the flour. Abbot Suger's verses, reappearing as far distant as St. Trophîme in Arles, explain the symbol;[25] however, it had nothing like the currency, iconographically, of the Melchisedec-Holy Supper parallel.

Petrarch as the First Modern Man first noticing the landscape on his famous mountain-climb, 'Moses looked at the view too'.

[25] See Mâle, *L'Art relig. du xiie siècle*, pp. 166 ff. and E. Panofsky, *Abbot Suger on the Abbey Church of St.-Denis*, Princeton, 1946 (for Suger's other types and symbols as well, influencing e.g. Godefroy de Claire—see my frontispiece, and other enamels, Mâle, p. 155). The grain-of-wheat symbolism is clear in Honorius's *Gemma animae*, i, ch. 31-32.

We see, then, that Herbert's *allegoria* in 'Peace' travels no unfrequented by-ways of the fancy, rather the broad high-road of accepted Christian symbolism. Of course, he does this in scores of poems, but since my point with this group of examples is the clear meaning and uneccentric character of certain apparently bizarre figures, I choose those most likely to impress a generation of readers like ourselves as singular, quaint, or—when this quality of strangeness goes 'too far' for the taste of this critic or that—forced and senti-mental. Another certain example is the 'Brave rose' of 'Church-rents and schismes' (p. 140), but here it is suffi-cient to remember the complete familiarity of all Christians of Herbert's time with the details of the allegorized Song of Solomon, so that Ecclesia as the 'rose' in the 'chair' or throne would not give the poem the almost wild strangeness it has for most readers now. A quality highly unsuitable, and not borne out by the metre or other formal factors. Another possible example is 'Justice, II' (p. 141).

If my own experience is at all typical, 'Justice, II' is powerful and clear in the first two stanzas, then with 'Christs pure vail presents the sight' (what sight?) and with the well-image it moves through two cloudy stanzas to a somewhat illogical conclusion: that since 'Gods pro-mises have made thee mine' (*thee* had up to now been God-as-Justice), I, Herbert, am safe in not *declining* Justice, since 'Against me there is none, but for me much'. These are the two middle stanzas:

> The dishes of thy ballance seem'd to gape,
>> Like two great pits;
>> The beam and scape
> Did like some torturing engine show;
> Thy hand above did burn and glow,
> Danting the stoutest hearts, the proudest wits.

But now that Christs pure vail presents the sight,
            I see no fears:
            Thy hand is white,
    Thy scales like buckets, which attend
    And interchangeably descend,
Lifting to heaven from this well of tears.

I think that this whole poem depends on the image, originally Augustinian and Gregorian and hence likely to be common property, of the Cross as a balance, the scales of God's judgement. The awful inadequacy of man before God as Justice, administering the Law, is what gives the first two stanzas their terror and power, and an element of unstated contrast between the old dispensation and the new lies behind the poem, as so often. The basic visual element in the patristic image is generally the Cross as a balance with cross-beam and scape; the basic concept is the weigh, ing by the just Father of man's sins in one dish against the sufferings of Christ as Man—so that when the Crucifixion took place the sufferings in their dish completely out, weighed the sins, and the *just* verdict can be in favour of man's salvation. The notion of the unceasing re-enactment of these events, presented with such poignancy by both Donne and Herbert, is clearest in the two buckets waiting and descending for their freight of *peccata* and *calamitas* to be lifted to heaven from 'this well of tears' in an incessant suc, cession of merciful unbalancings. The iconography of this, for it was vivid but rare as a graphic image, has been handled by F. Wormald, giving various patristic quota, tions.[26] Hence I need not go into it except to suggest that

[26] In *Journal of the Warburg and Courtauld Institutes*, i (1937–8), 276–80, with plates; the bucket-like two dishes of the Cross-balance recall Herbert's words. For 'Augustine's' Meditations next-mentioned see *Patr. Lat.* 40: 908, ch. viii, and Part I above, n. 28; for Wormald's Bernard reference see *Patr. Lat.* 184: 972; for the Anselm–Bernard reference I add see *Patr. Lat.* 184: 962. These attribu, tions are all now seen as mistaken, but the late Renaissance reader could read in

perhaps Augustine appears as a sort of sponsoring figure
(with Gregory and ? Bernard) in the miniatures described
because the image of our sin being outweighed by the good/
ness of the Saviour appears in the Meditations ascribed to
Augustine, which I have cited so often. Wormald quotes
the image from an Easter Monday sermon attributed (how/
ever mistakenly) to St. Bernard—certainly a favoured author
in the late Renaissance if numerousness of editions be any
guide. Another 'sermon of St. Bernard's on the Passion' is
Englished by R. B. in a book entitled amusingly enough
The yong mans gleanings (1614). This 'sermon' is the so/
called *Stimulus amoris* which appeared often as Anselm's
during the Renaissance, and as Bernard's; it also contains
the image of the balance with our 'sins' outweighed by the
'calamity' Christ suffered, and the context is like Herbert's
a prayer to the Father from whom we have deserved that
He should pour 'the vials of his ire' (p. 78) upon us. This
was a popular text, and contains several other images of
Herbert's which I treat.[27] Moreover, an image must be
thought of as familiar when it not only appears in Gregory's
Moralia but is commented on, with patristic quotations, in
the great standard glossed Bible: '. . . statera id est Cristus
. . .', s.v. Job vi.

The image is treated with some elaboration and con/
nected with the sign Libra, the Balance, in a kind of
heavenly zodiac described in Guillaume de Deguileville's
Pilgrimage of the Soul. This book was printed with wood/

plenty of places what *he* thought these three great writers had written on the
Cross as Balance.

[27] The Delectable Face which angels desire to see, spat upon; the payment for
what was never taken; the organs conceit; Joseph's coat. See above Part I, notes
26, 15, and below n. 34. Though Dom Wilmart now questions the attribution
(*Les Auteurs spirituels . . .*, 1932, pp. 173 ff.), this appeared many times as ch. ix
of the Meditations ascribed to Anselm; I give the *incipit* because of the confusing
early ascriptions: 'Jesum Nazarenum a Judaeis innocenter. . . .' On glossed
Bibles see the Note on accessibility of materials at the end of this book.

cuts by Vérard, translated by Caxton, and there are numerous manuscripts, though Lydgate's translation stops short of this portion. It happens to contain also a very vivid use of Christ as the apple on the Tree of the Cross. Christ the Sun of Righteousness travels through an allegorized zodiac (Aquarius: Baptism; Taurus: Herod, &c.) and enters upon the sign of the Balance: 'Upon the balance of the cross there was the treasure weighed that must be paid for the ransom of Adam's lineage; there was never gold nor silver so busily examined, for they enforced him so sore to the weight till the cords bursted of the balance, that were the sinews and veins of his blessed body . . .' (I merely modernize Caxton). I do not mention such a popularization of the patristic image because I think Herbert knew this specific one, although there was nothing to prevent it. I think he took this image from learned sources. But such examples illustrate the filtering through of symbols, that process by which a 'tradition' *is* carried. It was a process by which Herbert benefited and to which he contributed, though it is no longer operating in a lively way in the area here dealt with.

Herbert could, then, still count on readers who took his meaning without any sense of oddity when he said, after a sharply visualized description of great towering scales, 'But now that *Christs pure vail presents* the sight'. Christ's 'veil, that is to say, his flesh', says Heb. x. 20, read during the Passion season. Christ and His Cross *are* the scales, and though under the Law God called on man fearfully for Justice, now under the new promises which have made Christ his *he* can call for and be saved by the operation of that very justice he feared. 'Why should I justice now decline?' This *veil* is, of course, in itself another symbol of the thematic contrast between the Old and New Dispensation; Christ's flesh is as the veil before the tabernacle, and he is

the new and living way by which we approach (Heb. ix,
x). Herbert means exactly what he says, and it is a very
clear statement: the Body of Christ *presents* the scales of
judgement, now happily in man's favour.

This clarity, and the living and moving transformation
of a powerful image before our eyes, as it takes on the
weight of element after element in the poem's meaning,
makes a much better poem of 'Justice, II'. In feeling, the
image is closest perhaps to the most familiar of all uses of
the Cross as Balance—in Venantius Fortunatus' *Vexilla
regis prodeunt. Statera facta est corporis*, says this hymn, repeatedly sung in the Passion season, appearing in all editions of Fortunatus complete and incomplete, and in
Renaissance anthologies of Christian Latin poetry like that
of Fabricius. 'O beautiful and luminous tree . . . on whose
mystic arms hath hung   The whole world's ransom;
made a scale,   That fell to victim's side and flung   Safe,
toward heaven, the prey of hell.' It occurs also in a sequence
printed by Clichtoveus as Adam of St. Victor's: 'On the
cross' scales lifted   Christ was there extended   As the
price expended'; 'Crux est nostrae   Libra iustitiae'. And
if Herbert intended a pun on *scala*, as the notes suggest, the
Cross was both ladder and balance in this sequence, and
Christ Himself can be called either.[28]

I shall give but one more example of imagery which if
it is familiar rather than strange is lifted out of the category
of the odd, the *recherché*, or the eccentric. We may then
pass on to examples which have become actual puzzles
because of our lack of knowledge of traditional figurative

---

[28] *Salve crux arbor vitae*, for the Exaltation of the Cross; tr. by Wrangham, no.
lxxvi. On the 16th-cent. liturgiologist Clichtoveus, author of the most considerable Renaissance collection and critical commentary of liturgical poetry,
see the Note on accessibility of these materials. 'Et ideo Christus inter coelum et
terram scalam faciebat', says the *Speculum hum. salv.*, making Christ Jacob's
Ladder (33; Ascension).

language. This one example is in 'Whitsunday' (p. 59); since the first riddle or puzzle occurs there too it will be convenient to treat the two together and not break up the poem.

Herbert's 'Whitsunday' fails of its effect for most modern readers. This is partly because we are less interested than he in its subject-matter, the transmission of the Spirit's light and fire to the Gentiles and the dimming of that light in seventeenth-century England, but partly also because we cannot grasp its peculiar images with ease and pleasure, and hence cannot translate it into anything meaningful to ourselves. Herbert's 'Where is that fire?' is a question asked by our poets too, but however we may need a new Pentecost we cannot read of it in Herbert's poem when we can scarcely find the old one there. The puzzling image is the pipes of gold, and the odd one is that fancy of the sun, outshone, seeing 'twelve sunnes for one   Going about the world, and giving light'. The tissue into which both are woven consists of two strands: a symbolism of brilliant light and a symbolism of fructifying and redeeming water.

The connexion of both of these with the Holy Spirit is important to recall here, however hackneyed. Use of the first would be natural to anyone, on the feast when there descended upon the apostles the flames, the tongues, that made possible the extension of the Church. It is the feast when, as Durandus says, actual flames were scattered from the roof in some churches, or flowers, 'for joy', or doves let loose. Actually Herbert plays a fugue upon themes which are the great words and concepts played upon with endless variety in the liturgy of this season: *light, love, gift, joy*. The ceaseless invocations to light, the flames of *caritas*, the Seven Gifts of the Holy Ghost, the Gift as proper name for the Third Person—these are the themes of the sequences and hymns of the Whitsun season. The liturgical poems are numerous, since (in the Anglican Church too) Monday and Tuesday are feast days, and Wednesday, Friday, and Saturday are Ember Days; and they are not obscure pieces, but are some of the most widely known and justly famous of Christian poems. One of them is the sole medieval hymn to find a place in the Anglican Book of Common Prayer; the *Veni creator spiritus* there used in the office for the ordering of priests has these same themes: *donum Dei, Fons vivus, ignis, caritas . . . Accende lumen sensibus, Infunde amorem cordibus . . . Da gaudiorum praemia . . . .* Some of the best-known others are Adam of St. Victor's *Lux jucunda, lux insignis,* his *Simplex in essentia,* and the beautiful *Veni Sancte Spiritus Et emitte caelitus   Lucis tuae radium . . .',* with its striking *O lux beatissima.*[29] Herbert's brilliantly lighted stanzas thus take their place among many others, with the 'glorious gifts' that made earth seem like a heaven, and the stars coming down to serve here.

But the symbolism of water is not to be disconnected from all this. The Dove of Pentecost came down over the waters of the Jordan at Christ's Baptism, and in part Herbert's 'cordiall water' typifies baptism into the Church. But the liturgy for this week continually combines with the light-bringing symbol that of water for spiritual life, in connexion with the apostles' mission. 'Thou quickenest . . . water . . . to ransom souls . . . revive hearts . . . with spiritual life'; 'let the sacred quire . . . the promised joys sound forth . . . sun and moon . . . earth . . . glittering stars' all in concert join; 'Then forth they [the apostles] go, a light amid the gloom,   Dropping the word's good seed . . . While the supernal dew   Blesses the thirsty new-sown field'; 'Thou, working in the water pure, mysterious virtue dost assure to bless thy chosen race . . . Thou art the gift, the giver, too'. All of these were to be read in the Sarum Missal. In others mentioned above the apostles 'rain down ferti﹣lizing words';[30] in Augustine's treatment of Ps. 77 the turning of the apostles to the Gentiles is a fulfilling of God's threat in Isa. v. 6, that he will command the clouds to drop no more rain upon the Jews his vineyard. Adam of St. Victor's sequence for the apostles Peter and Paul calls them glittering clouds, watering the earth of the heart, now with dew, now with rain. In the sequence for the Common of an Apostle in the Sarum Use the apostles are like heavenly luminaries; they are the candlesticks before God's face. In that for Saints Peter and Paul, these are 'those true lights of heaven who cast their golden gleams o'er the world'.

Herbert's apostles as 'twelve sunnes . . . Going about the world, and giving light' is thus scarcely an eccentric image; moreover, there is a closer and more definite connexion than we might realize between traditional emphases and Herbert's next lines:

> But since *those pipes of gold, which brought*
> *That cordiall water* to our ground,
> Were cut and martyr'd by the fault
> Of those, who did themselves through their side wound,
>
> Thou shutt'st the doore, and keep'st within;
> Scarce a good joy creeps through the chink: . . .

Hutchinson's notes quite correctly cite in connexion with these extraordinary apostles﹣as﹣golden﹣conduits the verses in Zech. iv. 11–14: 'What are these two olive trees . . . these

---

[30] Relevant but, of course, not the same is the extremely conventional metaphor of the four evangelists as the four rivers of Paradise—in Jerome, in Augustine, in Durandus's and others' treatises, in art, in the poems of any and every one. Quotations above are from the sequences for, respectively, Whit Sunday; Whit Monday; Tuesday of Whit week (when incidentally Herbert read out the 'door' parable of John x; see the next quotation); Ember Wednesday (the *Lux jucunda*).

two olive branches which through the two golden pipes empty the golden oil out of themselves? . . . that stand by the Lord of the whole earth?' This is part of a vision concerning the foundation of Zerubabbel—a type of the true Church, which God says shall be established 'Not by might, nor by power, but *by my spirit*'. The figure recurs in Rev. xi. 4: 'These are the two olive trees, and the two candlesticks [candles] standing before the God of the earth'; and the prophet's question 'what are these two?' was not left unanswered in the liturgy of the church. The apostles Peter and Paul are the two olive-trees, the two golden pipes, the two candlesticks. 'Twin beauteous olive trees they stand before the Lord   Bright candlesticks which shed celestial light abroad,   Twin lamps which gleamed around the firmament afar', says the hymn (*Aurea luce*) in the Sarum Breviary for the vigil of these saints.[31] The Gradual sung in Sarum Use for these two apostles (octave) and for Saints John and Paul is the 'two olive trees . . . two candles' verse from Revelation.

The existence of a traditional connexion between apostles and the gold pipes of the O.T. vision makes our reading of Herbert's image a certainty instead of a fairly risky guess. I do not believe he would have made these curious connexions had the traditional allegorization not existed; grant the mere suggestion from the above liturgical sources or elsewhere, and we have his own word for it that he enjoyed the kind of connecting of Bible verses which here ties Zech. and Rev. (see 'H. Scriptures', p. 58). Apostles as gold pipes bringing to the Gentiles the life-giving water of baptism into a Church established on the first Whit Sunday,

---

[31] If this seems out-of-the-way reading, the hymn is printed as by Rabanus Maurus (p. 76) in the handsome Brouwer edition of Venantius Fortunatus mentioned in the Note on accessibility; printed also in the early school-books entitled *Expositio hymnorum* and in Clichtoveus, with commentary; there was a folio edition of Rabanus in 1627.

'cut and martyr'd' like Christ by those who did not know they thus cut themselves, cut and martyred again by schisms within the Church—Herbert's image is now clear enough, and it becomes quite natural that he proceeds to 'Lord, though we change, thou art the same . . . Restore this day . . . Unto his ancient and miraculous right'.

Like many riddles, this one took more investigation than it had a right to expect. What we have done in studying this image differs from what we had been doing heretofore, and it has produced a different result. We have merely cleared up a tough spot; we have not as in former instances provided a whole new dimension of meaning, or perceived how the wit of long-familiar metaphors was simultaneously potent and unobtrusive. For this image is not such a one, and I honestly do not think Herbert should have used it. To be sure it probably offered no such enigma in his day as it does to us, but the gap is patent between this narrow conceit and the light and water symbolism of the rest of the poem. Those are symbols which still carry their burden of Illumination and Purgation, Enkindling and Fruitfulness, and are meaningful even outside a Christian context. It is almost always the case that the greater symbols, which show this living fecundity and this tendency to lead the thought into reaches beyond those seen by the user, are the symbols whose long history had made them the familiar inheritance of the Western Christian mind. They were strong and durable because they had deep roots, and remain fecund for the same reason.

This whole language was at Herbert's disposal and largely intelligible still, in its Christian context, to his readers; he was not in the dilemma of modern poets and was not as they are practically forced into the use of symbols that are all but private. In Yeats's case an honest poet had to reject traditional patterns of symbols as not meaningful

to him, had then to search out, recombine, create new patterns—a herculean task that deserves our deepest respect. In
Eliot's case private allusiveness has given place to the use
of traditional patterns not obscure once but obscure at this
date in history—an attempt at rehabilitation that again deserves our esteem. Other poets have turned to Freudian
psychology as offering almost the only modern pattern
whose basic symbols have become 'second nature' to literate
readers. Herbert did not labour under these difficulties. To
be quite fair to him, he does not often use images, like these
golden pipes, which require that we should put our fingers
almost upon his very source, follow in the footsteps of his
working mind. What we have done is analogous to what
a modern critic does when he studies certain puzzling locutions of Eliot's *Four Quartets* by adducing quotations from
Elyot's *Governour*, or what Yeats does when he explains to
us his reference to Jacques Molay in 'Meditations in Time
of Civil War'. It is necessary, and it helps the poem, in all
three cases.

To be sure, Herbert has substituted this passage for one
containing an image that would have given modern readers
troubles whose results I shudder to contemplate. The Williams MS. has a form of the image of God's breasts: 'Show
that thy brests can not be dry,   But that from them ioyes
purle for ever   Melt into blessings all the sky . . .' (part of
an alternative section asking, as does the one printed, for
God's rejuvenating grace upon His Church). Herbert uses
it again in 'Longing' (p. 148), a poem addressed to 'Lord
Jesu': 'From thee all pitie flows.   Mothers are kinde,
because thou art,   And dost dispose   To them a part:
Their infants, them; and they suck thee.' These are no
riddles, but conventional images. Stemming primarily from
the Song of Solomon, traditional allegory connects the breasts
especially with *caritas* (even with its two traditional pre-

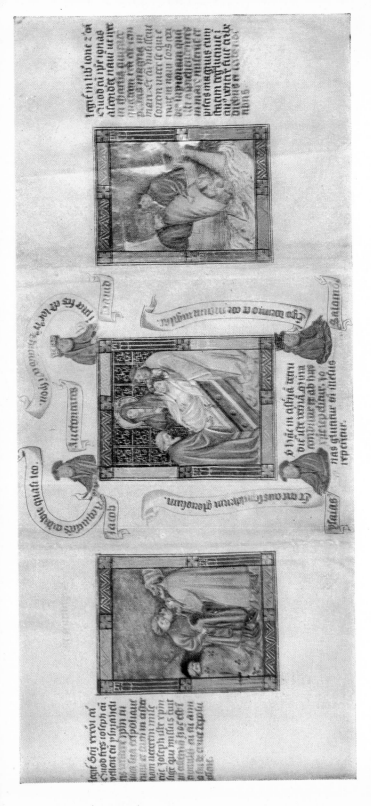

Colour Plate I

Biblia Pauperum, B.Mus. MS. King's 5, f. 19ʳ, c. 1400: Joseph's coat, Entombment, Jonah

cepts) and with *doctrine* (the 'milk of doctrine', 'milk of consolation'), and endlessly mentions the two Testaments.[32] The image was probably excised from the Whitsun poem because its language is not, like that of 'Longing', the language of the mystical love between the soul and Christ. But the fitness in both contexts (Christ as fountain of all love; the Holy Spirit giving spiritual food, the apostles carrying doctrine) is clear enough; and the ease with which breasts: love: doctrine can be either the Church's or God's is not unusual and is part of the strength of allegory.

Three other 'riddles' or puzzles are the only remaining images of Herbert's which I shall discuss. Two of these three provide readings with which I am not entirely satisfied, but at least they help to explain a poem that would otherwise be vapid and inexplicably titled, and a passage in a familiar poem—'Church-musick'—that otherwise makes sense only by guesswork. The first image forms the title of a poem, and the important thing is that if we give it the traditional interpretation the substance of the poem is quite transformed.

Why did Herbert call the poem on p. 159 'Josephs coat'?

[32] See Durandus, Sunday after Easter; we now read the apostles that we may be 'allaités . . . Car les Écritures sont les mamelles dont il est dit . . .' (quotes *Cant. cant.* i. 2); the Lord comforts us by that food. I do not go into the interpretations which can be found in various treatises, but e.g. in Honorius, *Expos. Cant. cant.*, *Patr. Lat.* 172: 361–4, the relation of all this to *anima* as spouse and to the Holy Spirit, even to the 'milk' of such doctrines as the seven Gifts of the Holy Ghost, can be examined. See *A Little Pamphlet of St. Augustine entitled the Ladder of Paradise* (STC 937; listed with long commendatory title by Maunsell in his 1595 *Catalogue*); it says speaking of Christ, 'suck milk and honey out of the breast of his consolation' (*Scala paradisi*, ch. vi, *Patr. Lat.* 40: App.). Alabaster uses it in a sonnet. For a striking portrayal of two elders nourished at the breasts of Ecclesia see the Bourges Apocalypse window, Plate 20b in *Journal of Warburg and Courtauld Institutes*, xi (1948). Even the late American Puritan Jonathan Edwards makes this § 113 of his *Images or Shadows of Divine Things* (ed. Perry Miller, New Haven, 1948; see §§ 90, 108, 56, 80 for other parallels with images I discuss).

What became of Joseph, after the title? Why *coat* at all, why does it reappear in the poem as Joy's coat, enticed 'to linger in me', and when did God 'give to anguish one of Joyes coats'?

Joseph's coat has a very definite meaning in Christian symbolism; any among a dozen treatises will give it, or the glossed Bibles, for it occurs in the *Glossa ordinaria*, in Lyra, Hugo de S. Charo, and the *Bibles moralisées*. Next to Moses, Joseph was the most familiar of the more general types for Christ, especially in the arts, and the two high points in the parallel, iconographically, are Christ in the tomb (Joseph put into the *cisterna*) and the *tunica* shown to the Father with the words 'Wild beasts have devoured him'. Quite aside from glass, sculpture, &c., this parallel was again one of those nailed into people's visual memories by being universally included in typological series in printed books and late manuscripts. The *Biblia Pauperum* and the illustrated *Horae* and Books of Christian Prayers give two cuts to parallels between Christ and Joseph (Entombment, set beside Joseph put into the round brick well; the Marys seeking Christ, beside Reuben seeking Joseph; both sets are in the typological windows Herbert saw often at King's College, Cambridge). The *Speculum humanae salvationis* discusses at length the parallels between Joseph's coat and Christ's.[33] The children of Jacob tore Joseph's coat, the Jews tore Christ's flesh with nails and thorns; Joseph's coat felt no pains, the body of Christ felt pain in every member; Joseph's coat reached to the heels, in Christ from His crown to His heels no well place appeared; the brothers of Joseph sprinkled Joseph's coat with the blood of a kid, but the Jews sprinkled Christ's

[33] Anyone interested in the matter from the point of view of source study proper could make a very good case for Herbert's familiarity specifically with the text of the *Speculum*, as will be apparent if my instances are classified and studied.

XVI *a. Speculum hum. salv.*, Bodl. MS. Douce 204, f. 26ʳ, xv c.;
Deposition, Joseph's coat

XVI *b. Speculum hum. salv.*, B.Mus. MS. Harl. 2838, f. 28ᵛ, xv c.:
Deposition Joseph's coat

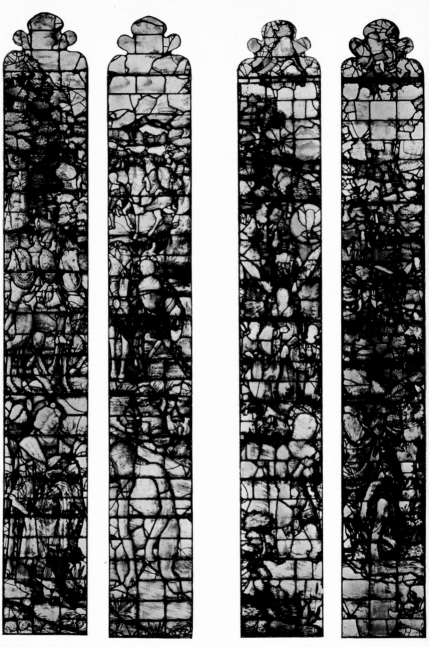

XVII. King's College Chapel, Cambridge, window VII north: Naaman, Baptism

'coat' with his own blood. The pictures show the Deposi﹢
tion from the Cross paralleled by the showing of the blood﹢
stained tunic to Jacob. (See Plates XVI *a*, *b*, and Colour
Plate I—a manuscript *BP* substituting Entombment for
Deposition. The other two *Speculum* parallels, not repro﹢
duced, are Adam and Eve grieving over the dead Abel,
and Naomi weeping.)

We must remember that these iconographical sources
portray not newly invented parallels but commonplaces.
The pictures of the brothers holding up the tunic before
their aged father are striking, and once one (knowing the
parallel) has seen this episode juxtaposed to the wounded
Christ of the Deposition, it is very hard to think of 'Josephs
coat' without thinking also of the Crucifixion. The parallel
is in Antony de Rampegollis's handbook of biblical figures
(under *De resurr.*). The popular Passion meditation men﹢
tioned earlier, which was printed both as Anselm's and as
Bernard's, says of the crucified Christ: 'Take knowledge
(O Father) unto the coat of thy true sonne Joseph . . . a
savage beast hath devoured him, and trampled uppon his
garment . . . staining his bewtie . . . behold he hath made
pitifull rents in it.'[34] There follows the parallel with Joseph's
other coat, the one left behind in the grasp of Potiphar's
wife; Christ too chose rather to be despoiled of the garment
of his flesh. The glosses and commentators explain the
tunica of Gen. xxxvii. 23 as *humanitas Christi*. Joseph's coat
was the *humanity* of Christ which he put on to save man,
and of which he was 'denuded' or 'despoiled' by those he
was to save, like the earlier redemptive hero, Joseph. This

---

[34] From p. 76 of R. B.'s version quoted above (see note 27 and text); for Latin
passage see *Patr. Lat.* 184: 961. Or see *Bernard his . . . Sighes, Sobbes, & Teares*,
STC 1919, 1921, pp. 235, 212, respectively. Mâle, *L'Art relig. de la fin du m. âge*,
p. 143, cites S. Bonaventura's *Tree of the Cross* (Fr. translation, end of 15th
cent., printed by S. Vostre). The treatise by Hugo mentioned in this para﹢
graph is in *Patr. Lat.* 175; see cols. 651–2.

appears everywhere, from Isidore on Genesis to the *Glossa ordinaria*, or Rabanus's *Allegoriae* (s.v. *tunica*), or Hugo of St. Victor's *Allegoriae in vetus Testamentum*.

Against this background, I do not believe we can think that a puzzling title 'Josephs coat' can have been picked out of the air, for no reason explained in the body of the poem, by a poet who shows Herbert's familiarity with other such symbols. If he had used this title with the innocent and weakly haphazard meaning suggested in Hutchinson's note he would certainly have given a very false lead to readers who had any of that knowledge of allegorical commonplaces which he himself expects of them all through the rest of his poems. I think that the poem's theme is close to that of 'The Crosse' (p. 164) and 'Affliction, III' (p. 73); and I believe that, as in the first-named,[35] the title serves to indicate a common Christian idea, 'Take up My Cross...' —i.e. the eternal repetition, in men, of Christ's struggle, in the coat of his flesh, with the anguish which is the other side of all human joy.

Josephs coat

Wounded I sing, tormented I indite,
    Thrown down I fall into a bed, and rest:
Sorrow hath chang'd its note: such is his will,
    Who changeth all things, as him pleaseth best.
        For well he knows, if but one grief and smart
    Among my many had his full career,
        Sure it would carrie with it ev'n my heart,
    And both would runne untill they found a biere
        To fetch the bodie; both being due to grief.
But he hath spoil'd the race; and giv'n to anguish

[35] Notice the use of the 'taken up and thrown down' image in both poems, probably punningly in 'Josephs coat' when the *bed* is mentioned, for physical illness is one of the 'griefs' in all this group of poems. This image is from one of the Seven Penitential Psalms (102); hence the fitness of a variant of it in Donne's 'Batter my heart'.

One of Joyes coats, ticing it with relief
To linger in me, and together languish.
I live to shew his power, who once did bring
My *joyes* to *weep*, and now my *griefs* to *sing*.

'Affliction, III' has the revealing and pertinent passage:
'Thy life on earth was grief, and thou art still   Constant
unto it, making it to be   A point of honour, *now to grieve
in me,   And in thy members suffer ill* . . . Thou dying dayly
. . .' (cf. above, 'To linger in me . . .'). 'Wounded I sing,
tormented I indite', begins 'Josephs coat', and it is pertinent
to remember Herbert's use of the conceit of Love singing
on the Cross, though Love is at that moment Grief Incarnate. God 'once did bring   My *joyes* to *weep*'—Christ
was the very body of Joy in 'Love-joy' (p. 116). 'And now
my *griefs* to *sing*'; compare the music conceit, and in a poem
related to and just preceding 'Josephs coat' God weeps the
one tear of Christ's bloody struggle and the poet sings
because the bottle of tears he has been unable to fill is thus
suddenly full to overflowing. In 'The Reprisall', too (p. 36),
God has outgone the poet in griefs through the sufferings
of the Passion; compare the idea in 'Josephs coat' that God
hath spoiled the race (in which any one of Herbert's griefs
would have killed him, heart and body) by winning it
already, giving over *Humanitas Christi*, our joy incarnate, to
the anguish of the Passion, but also uniting His Son with
man in their common humanity, 'ticing' this *humanitas
Christi* to remain in man and for ever transform both his joy
and his grief.[36] The last two lines are now a true conclusion.

The sonnet is certainly stronger and deeper when thus
read as a poignant attempt to see and phrase the relation

---

[36] Or, indifferently, spoiled the race grief would have won, by dressing the
greatest grief of all, the Passion, in that joy which must be its aspect to those who
were saved by Christ's taking on humanity. I would note that without this
symbolic extension the 'joy' comes from nowhere and has no meaning.

between joy and grief, rather than as a pale comment on their juxtaposition. As a poem praising God for His psychological acuteness in so neat an arrangement it has next to no poetic stature. It was written by a human being who found all but impossible the necessary 'In thy will is our peace'. I may have over-read it; all that is required may be the hint of relation between Christ and Joseph's coat, but I think the conception 'he in us and we in him' is also necessary. That Herbert could not have missed knowing this commonplace of Christian symbolism and that he used it to deepen his poem's significance, I am entirely sure; of my interpretation of that deepening I am not sure.

The passage in 'Church-musick' for which no one has ever found an explanation occurs when Herbert suddenly breaks off a description of the very sensation of listening to music with the ejaculation, 'God help poore Kings'.

> Sweetest of sweets, I thank you: when displeasure
>   Did through my bodie wound my minde,
> You took me thence, and in your house of pleasure
>   A daintie lodging me assign'd.
>
> Now I in you without a bodie move,
>   Rising and falling with your wings:
> We both together sweetly live and love,
>   Yet say sometimes, *God help poore Kings*.

(p. 65; italics Herbert's)

God help the poor reader, for no reason is to be seen else-where in the poem for the entrance of these kings, and no annotator has brought forward any satisfactory explanation of such writing on the part of a poet so careful. I offer one explanation, for whatever it is worth.

The only psalm which is entirely about music sung by the Church of God in His praise is Ps. 149, *Cantate Domino canticum novum: laus eius in ecclesia sanctorum.* The congregation of saints (i.e. 'the Church') is through several verses adjured to sing, with praises in their mouth and a two-edged sword in their hands; the eighth verse, telling what they shall do with this sword, reads: 'To *bind their kings in chains*: and their nobles with links of iron.' 'Such honour have all his saints', the meek-hearted congregation of the faithful. This psalm, with the almost as music-filled 148 and 150, held an imposing place: in that *Dirige* which gave the English language its word *dirge*, i.e. in the Office for the Dead (Lauds) that was printed scores of times in Books of Hours and Primers. We should remember per-haps that Herbert has been fancying his soul separated from his body, and that he continues 'Comfort, I'le die; . . . But if I travell in your companie,   You know the way to heavens doore'. His poem was written in a time of illness, and as one of the Church of God being told to sing he may have got some of the amusement we do from being adjured 'let them rejoice *in their beds*'. Verse 8 was made an anti-phon, slightly rephrased ('Alliga Domine in vinculis . . . reges eorum in compedibus'); it was thus sung alone— during Holy Week. The vengeful fierceness towards kings of this singing Church of the faithful provides a connexion I do not know except here and in Herbert; no psalm would be more a part of common language (unless perhaps the Penitential Psalms and those for Matins),[37] and certainly it

[37] Out of the great mass of the psalms, certain groups (besides those for Matins and Evensong) stood out by virtue of centuries of special attention: the Seven Penitential Psalms, the Fifteen Gradual Psalms, the psalms found in the Primer or *Horae*, and the psalms which were accompanied by illuminations in the Psalter because they began the divisions into nocturns, for Matins. We are not always aware of the extent to which locutions and images in these especially familiar 'hymns' have left their colour on the language; when a Lady Anne Clifford, for example, speaks of being 'an owl in the desert', in a *Diary* that contains scarcely an image, she is not being suddenly inventive but quite naturally echoing one of the Penitential Psalms (102). Walton says Herbert would explain the 'Psalms and Lauds' of the services to his parishioners. In Sarum Use, Ps. 149 would have been said every Sunday (Common for Lauds).

was a *locus classicus* for 'Church-musick'. It is one of the seven psalms which Bacon translated and dedicated to Herbert in 1625.

This last example is different from the others examined in that the element of symbolism involved is very minor, if present. It is correspondingly unimportant. It is when ex-planations allow us to see into the nature of metaphors, which are a poet's only way of telling the truth, that they are important.

§4. *'Jordan'*

The last example of an image of Herbert's whose riddle is unravelled by a knowledge of traditional Christian symbols will explain finally and satisfactorily, I think, the puzzling titles of two of his poems which have been much quoted as showing his attitude towards the Metaphysical style, and towards secular love poetry. What is more important, a better understanding of these two poems will illuminate some seven or eight others whose interrelations are revealing, and the process will serve to uncover basic elements in Herbert's poetic theory, which in turn are inextricable from his conceptions of the significance of human life. These matters have much to do with the reasons why his work has still a living and poignant unity.

The first poem in 'The Church' (following 'The Church-porch') is 'The Altar'—'a broken Altar, made of a heart'. Like all poets of both sacred and profane love, Herbert plays many variations on the motif of the heart as stone, and usually we detect the influence of two favourite ancient conceits: the heart as the *sepulchrum* in which the body of Christ is placed and thus His tabernacle; and the heart of flesh that is the Table of Stone whereon the new Law, of

love, is inscribed, thus again representing God's tabernacle.
The two conceits meet in 'Sepulchre', p. 40. These turns
of thought are not absent from 'The Altar', but the chief
influence upon the metaphor which constitutes the poem
is a passage in Deut. xxvii. 2-9. It is an impressive passage,
in which Moses proclaims to all Israel, 'This day thou art
become the people of the Lord thy God', and in which he
describes with care an altar, not one he will build, but one
that is to be built: 'And it shall be on the day when ye shall
pass over Jordan.' It is the altar which is to mark trium-
phantly the end of the Oppression and of the long wander-
ing in the desert, and it has one salient characteristic, a
characteristic to be significantly allegorized by Herbert.

Therefore it shall be *when ye be gone over Jordan*, that ye shall set
up these stones . . . and thou shalt plaister them with plaister.
And there shalt thou build . . . an altar of stones: *thou shalt not
lift up any iron tool upon them* . . . And thou shalt offer burnt
offerings thereon unto the Lord thy God.

'No workmans tool hath touch'd the same', says Herbert;
'A HEART alone   Is such a stone,   As nothing but
Thy pow'r doth cut'. The stone has been 'plaistered'
('cemented with teares'), but its 'parts are as thy hand did
frame'. The altar is described also in a passage forbidding
idolatry, in Exod. xx. 22 ff.; an altar of earth it is to be, or
if of stone not 'of hewn stone: for *if thou lift up thy tool upon
it*, thou hast polluted it'. Herbert's heart itself, 'these stones',
will praise God, 'if I chance to hold my peace'. The altar
which was to bear the offerings made for the fulfilment of
God's promise of salvation of the Chosen People, in the
Promised Land, was duly erected when they had crossed
over the Jordan which marked its boundary. It was duly
built of stones 'over which no man hath lift up any iron:
and they offered thereon burnt offerings' (Joshua viii. 31).

The Jordan whose crossing was already a symbol of redemption in the Old Testament became a yet more powerful one in the New, and the medieval Church widened and deepened its significances. As with many water symbols, its basic element is purification from sin, but its range of meanings becomes very great. The Chosen People, the Church of God, enter heaven and eternal life through the waters of Jordan; the single soul which in wedding Christ becomes His temple enters through its waters the joy of His eternal presence; its waters are the waters of baptism and this is the water that flowed from Christ's side, the regenerating and fructifying water; Christ's Baptism and Epiphany are paralleled and these are one with the wedding of Christ with His Church or with the soul. 'This day to a celestial spouse is joined the Church, because in Jordan Christ hath laved her sins', the Magi hasten with gifts to the royal nuptials, and the guests are made glad with water made wine—so says the antiphon for Sunday Lauds in Epiphany, Sarum Use. As Naaman was cleansed of his leprosy in the waters of Jordan, so Christ came to cleanse men from the leprosy of sin; Jordan 'signifies humility' by which the Church asks to be purified (Durandus, Bk. vi, ch. 47, as in Rabanus); Jordan's waves are a type of Ecclesia (Adam of St. Victor: *Jerusalem et Sion*); Jordan 'signifies Baptism'. This last is a commonplace occurring uncountable times in gloss and commentary.

Before we turn to Herbert's poems 'Jordan, I' and 'Jordan, II' the two-part poem entitled 'Love' claims our attention, although we must refer again to 'Love', I and II, when the content of the Jordan poems is more fully before us. For the Jordan poems have two themes, and one is the building 'on the day when ye shall pass over Jordan' of this altar of the heart's pure love unpolluted by the touch of any workman's tool; the other, if it can be called other, is the consecration of the entire man to Heavenly Love as the prototype of all love, and a consequent dedication on Herbert's own part to sacred poetry. Herbert is no ascetic, and to say that these poems are 'a protest against love poems' is to stop at the very surface of their meaning; still less are they 'a protest against the pastoral allegorical poetry of the Cambridge Spenserians' (see Grierson's remarks quoted in Hutchinson's notes). Nor is the famous 'Catching the sense at two removes', in one of them, a protest against the Meta⁄ physical style. These poems are too large for such boxes; and although Herbert's theory of poetry is in them, it con⁄ sists of no such trivial objections to this or that group of writers, subject⁄matter or style.

In 'Love', Part II (p. 54), Herbert addresses Heavenly Love, which constructed and which will consume the world, and asks that it consume our imperfect kinds of love until our *hearts* speak it forth in their very heartbeats; then shall our *brain* 'All her invention on thine Altar lay, And there in hymnes send back thy fire again'. The title of 'Jordan, II' in the Williams MS. is *Invention*, and it de⁄ scribes certain ways in which Herbert thinks he went wide of the mark in his own earlier sacred poetry, 'When first [his] lines of heav'nly joyes made mention', i.e. when first he offered up his inventions to Heavenly Love. The judge⁄ ment he must make of these first 'bustling' poems is a harsh one: 'How wide is all this long *pretence*!' 'Jordan, II' is by far the most acute of the group in its self⁄examination, but it only uncovers a deeper and more hidden form of some⁄ thing he has seen and treated more simply in other poems— how he like other men treating of love has not had his eye on his great subject but upon a lesser something which he had erected in its place.

'Love', Part I, acclaims 'Immortall Love' as 'authour of this great frame', sprung from the fadeless and eternal Idea of Beauty; but half-blind man has parcelled out this 'glorious name', has given 'mortall love', the lesser reflection of that heavenly pattern, '*all* the title', 'thrown it on that dust which thou hast made'. This is the regular neo-Platonic cosmology with which we are familiar in Spenser (or in *Troilus*), and the error here pointed to is, as it almost always is in this framework of ideas, the substitution of the reflection for the reality, of the creature for the creator; *idolatry, not love, is the fault.* Mortal love 'siding with invention', they two 'Bear all the sway, possessing *heart* and *brain*', 'and give thee share in neither', though both are 'thy workmanship'. So poetry and human interchange becomes all one contest of 'wit' and praise of 'beautie', while all-creating Love stands left out of what has become mere sport and emulation— 'they two play out the game,   Thou standing by'. Although Love came down in person and 'wrought our deliverance from th'infernall pit', still we persist in this substitution of the creature for the Creator—'Who sings thy praise? onely a skarf or glove   Doth warm our hands, and make them write of love'. In Part II of 'Love' Herbert asks that this 'Immortall Heat', the 'greater flame', may 'attract the lesser to it', and the way of this is not the path of asceticism, but again the Spenserian way, the displacing of a dimmed and partial sight of the mere created part by a vision of the creating whole, 'Our eies shall see thee, which before saw dust'. Love perverted—lust—shall be replaced by love, and all wits shall 'praise him who did make and mend our eies'. God created the dust, but it is not He, and is not to be worshipped by either the loving heart or the ingenious brain—'Dust blown by wit, till that they both were blinde'. This is the setting for 'then shall our brain   All her invention on thine Altar lay'—the altar of Love itself—and the poem is not a protest against human love but against its usurpation of the human heart.

Just so 'Jordan, 1' (p. 56) is not a protest against love poetry but against its usurpation of the whole field and very title of poetry.

> Who sayes that fictions onely and false hair
> Become a verse? Is there in truth no beautie?
> Is all good structure in a winding stair?
> May no lines passe, except they do their dutie
>   Not to a true, but painted chair?
>
> Is it no verse, except enchanted groves
> And sudden arbours shadow course-spunne lines?
> Must purling streams refresh a lovers loves?
> Must all be vail'd, while he that reades, divines,
>   Catching the sense at two removes?
>
> Shepherds are honest people; let them sing:
> Riddle who list, for me, and pull for Prime:
> I envie no mans nightingale or spring;
> Nor let them punish me with losse of rime,
>   Who plainly say, *My God, My King*.

'Let them sing', he says of love poets (the shepherds who wrote in eclogue, lyric, elegy, pastoral, all the small secular kinds); they are honest people, he casts no aspersions on any man's choice of nightingale or spring—he says 'I *envie* not', with the seventeenth-century force of begrudge not, cavil not at, as the surrounding words show. For himself, he claims the right to prefer another kind of good structure than that in a winding stair, means to declare in his verses his allegiance to majesty itself and not the image of it, to the true and not the painted throne.[38] And, seeing beauty in

---

[38] The neo-Platonic character of Herbert's ideas of Heavenly Love may justify us in relating this to Plato's discussion of the artist's mere 'imitation' of the true in a painted table or bed, &c., in *Republic* x. Sidney's answer, in a doctrine of Imitation more Platonic than Plato's, shows the regular Renaissance neo-Platonic ground for conceptions of the relation between sacred and profane love poetry. With reference to the poem's last line: the piece in which Herbert

truth itself, essential and uncovered, he means to declare this allegiance as plainly and directly as he can. This is like the resolve he makes in 'Love', Part II, to lay the inventions of his brain on Love's altar and 'send back its fire again' in the burnt offering of sacred hymns of praise. In each poem Herbert makes a personal dedication of his imagina‐ tion to Heavenly Love; but the dedication is made not without a touch of defiance and pride, and the problem is simply seen and simply solved.

By the time he writes 'Jordan, II' self‐criticism reaches into a much more profound level of the mind's workings. He is still concerned with the idolatry of substituting the shadows of beauty, truth, and love for their essential forms, but the idolatry he here detects is detected in himself rather than in others, and in one of the subtlest of all its forms— self‐love masquerading as self‐dedication. Milton has a similar insight in *Lycidas* and in certain comments on Stoic‐ ism, and Spenser's insight into self‐centredness as the basis of all perversions of the principle of Love in the human world covers and includes Herbert's.

'Jordan, II' (p. 102) is another consideration of how a man may make of his poetic imagination an offering to Heavenly Love. It is concerned not with the mere choice of sacred poetry but with the forms such poems take, and the way in which form can betray the inner lack of integrity in the poet. The word *Invention*, in the alternative title and in all uses in these poems, has the regular seventeenth‐ century rhetorical meaning: that which the imagination uncovers, finds, in the poet's search for a mode of bodying forth the unbodied conceptions of his mind. This is im‐

does certainly very 'plainly' (and three times) say 'My God and King' is 'An‐ tiphon, I' (p. 53). But dating is precarious, this antiphon is not in W., and we should be wary of conjecturing an origin for 'Jordan, I' in some stricture passed by an actual 'them' on Herbert's over‐simplicity. He argues chiefly with himself in his poems.

portant because the end of the poem tells the poet where to
look if he would be honest, and must not be misconstrued
as a sentimental injunction to attend to his simple feelings
and forget art. 'Jordan, II' describes earlier poems, dedicated
to Heavenly Love to be sure, but full of sought/for 'quaint
words, and trim invention', and of thoughts that burnished,
sprouted, and swelled, 'Curling with metaphors a plain
intention', 'Decking the sense, as if it were to sell'. Thinking
himself engrossed only in finding inventions rich enough
'to clothe the sunne', he had blotted and corrected, thrown
out this as not lively enough, and that as dead. At this
point, with one of those sudden changes of tone with which
Herbert so characteristically distinguishes a mental dis-
covery, he shows up his early busy obsession with the
effectiveness of his phrasings for what he now sees it to have
been—a gaze directed not upon love itself but upon his
successful eloquence in writing of it, not upon Christ but
upon the Poet Herbert.

> As flames do work and winde, when they ascend,
> So did I weave my self into the sense.
> But while I bustled, I might heare a friend
> Whisper, *How wide is all this long pretence!*
> *There is in love a sweetnesse readie penn'd:*
> *Copie out onely that, and save expense.*

'Expense of spirit', of course, with a glance at the thrift
of going directly to the fountain-head; Herbert is never
solemn in his self-accusations. So far is he from sentimentality that he can make a play upon his own serious
symbol of the burnt offering to God as Love, laid upon his
heart's altar: 'As flames do work and winde, when they
ascend,   So did I weave my self into the sense.' 'Weave
my self into' has two meanings. Nor does he share the com-
placent notion of Milton's Moloch that his proper motion

is ascent—descent and fall to him being adverse. The flames are his warm love (his very self) but also his love as burnt offering (selfless, a sacrifice), and the figure is for one thing an accurate description of the spiralling self-deceptions of the human psyche as it tries to 'ascend'. The image in these two lines is equally a statement of a fundamental human problem—the painful paradoxical attempt to lose the self in sacrifice, to devote the very personality without ceasing to be a person and yet without trace of self-interest or self-approbation. Herbert's solution of the paradox is not that of today's pseudo-psychologizing—all devotion is self-love in disguise, all service of the good at best a form of self-fulfilment, preserve the self at all costs, by way of looking to the good of others if feasible, but if not, at their cost. His solution is more daring. But the difficulties which have brought us to this sorry answer were no more hidden to him than to us, and the series of poems I am treating is the history of his advancing perception of them.

He here criticizes, then, not subtlety of metaphor nor richness of style but his own intellectual pride, in his own earlier writing. In the very act of dedicating himself to Christ as a soul cleansed of its love of the world he had been most interested in what flourishes his workman's tools could make on the stones of the altar. He can call those poems *Jordan* in which he sees at last what it means to build with stones unburnished, *lapidibus impolitis*,[39] and to burn and expend, not to take pride in, his offering.

He was quite right in thinking that he had crossed no Jordan at the time he erected the altar we read about in two still earlier 'Sonnets' on this same general subject. These he wrote when first he decided 'that my poor Abilities in

[39] This is the Vulgate phrase (Joshua viii. 31), and the offerings 'holocausta'. In Honorius, *Gemma animae*, i. 30, treating of the various types of offerings or sacrifices to God, *holocausta* are defined as those which consist of giving away all one has, the relinquishing of secular things.

Poetry, shall be all, and ever consecrated to Gods glory'. This comes from a letter sent to his mother, accompanying the sonnets, and they are as self-righteous as ever any poetry of a more worldly 17-year-old could be. 'My God ... Why are not *Sonnets* made of thee? and layes   Upon thine Altar burnt?' '*Roses* and *Lillies* speak thee' and it is an abuse to make a pair of cheeks of them, or to take women's eyes for crystal—'Such poor invention burns in their low mind   Whose fire is wild, and doth not upward go   To praise, and on thee, Lord, some *Ink* bestow.' (p. 206). The acuteness with which Herbert has turned this wild-weaving- fire image back upon himself in the later poem which we have just examined is wit in its truest sense; he clearly saw the comedy in his own youthful posing as an Abel to every other man's Cain.

Whether or not these two immature sonnets are being specifically referred to in his strictures on sought-for trim- ness of invention and decked-out sense, in 'Jordan, II', they assuredly fit that poem's diagnosis of what was wrong. The *sweetnesse readie penn'd* in the very nature of Love itself does not suit the young poet's book, for he is fully occupied in 'copying out' rather the shocking difference between other men's misdirected ardours and his own self-dedication. 'My God, where is that ancient heat towards thee?', whole shoals of Martyrs once burnt with it 'besides their other flames', yet now, though each breast feels the fire of love only 'by thy power and might', it chooses no braver fuel than that which one day worms may chance refuse. Can- not God's love heighten a spirit to sound out praises 'As well as any she?' These two sonnets sent to his mother as a New Year's gift in 1609/10 were quite properly not in- cluded in *The Temple*, and they and the letter are printed from Walton. The Magdalen Herbert whose sympathetic insight we know from Donne's poems would not be likely to miss any of the diverting aspects of being the Only She whom her young son could compliment under the label of to-be-rejected worm's meat.

To compare these with what I suppose is a redoing in the two sonnets entitled 'Love', Parts I and II, noting the similarity in several important ideas and in various con-ceits, is to make a study of the importance of tone in determining a poem's real subject—the early two could well have for title 'Of Myself'. It is also a study in what poetic maturity consists of. Nor has age alone conferred it upon Herbert; his poems record the difficulties of the process.

The true and complete absence of self-deceit which Her-bert achieves is achieved by rooting out of himself every vestige of self-seeking. It is because this process is, in his context of thought, the very functioning of Heavenly Love that we find several other poems as well whose subject is the relation between love of God and the writing of good poetry. If we think we have found in him a manifesto against fine style and over-subtlety, we must recall that he is quite as likely to berate himself because he seems *un*able to 'write fine and wittie'. He does this in both 'The Fore-runners' (p. 176) and in 'Dulnesse' (p. 115). The first defends 'Lovely enchanting language, sugar-cane,   Hony of roses' for the praises of God, in the same neo-Platonic context we have noted before; 'Beautie and beauteous words should go together' and human beauty is a flame borrowed from eternal beauty. So he complains against his dullness that has turned him to a clod, and indeed no reluctant farewell to lost power and sweetness was ever more meltingly phrased. But he wheels around on himself with the same careful distinction and the same answer as before; though his first impulse is to resent and question, his last is to look away from his own paltry judgements to what is real and central. 'Let a bleak palenesse chalk the doore', if only all within be more living than before.[40]

He charges himself with earth-like deadness in 'Dulnesse'—again in the context of neo-Platonic ideas of deity, for Christ is the Form, the idea itself of perfection and beauty, yet is Herbert outgone by the mere 'wanton lover' who in poems to his love can 'with quaint metaphors her curled hair   Curl o're again'. 'Where are *my* lines then? . . . Where are *my* window-songs?' If such lovers can be 'still pretending', continually urging their suits, if even wrongs sharpen *their* Muse, of what dull metal can such as he be made? Sure he is 'lost in flesh'; God 'put a minde there, if [he] could   Finde where it lies'. The contrast between all this and his youthful earlier conviction (stated in most hair-curling metaphors) that all men but he were lost in the toils of the flesh is very close to true comedy. He finds out the same cure as in 'Jordan, II'; in 'Dulnesse' he says: 'Lord, cleare thy gift' (his faulty, flesh-smothered mind) 'that *with a constant wit   I may but look towards thee'.* If he would look upon Love, the imitation thereof would be poetry; there is in love a sweetness ready penned, copy out only that. It is the Sidneian idea of poetry; the 'erected wit' must contemplate universals, then only do the great speaking images of poetry body them forth.

It is this element in Herbert's theory of poetry which gives it toughness, and makes safe such statements as that in 'A true Hymne' (p. 168): 'The *finesse* which a hymne or psalme affords,   Is, when the soul unto the lines accords.' (Fineness: subtlety or brave splendour, perhaps both.) He

---

[40] I cannot but suspect a connexion between the basic image of 'The Forerunners' and the familiar symbol of the *tau* (supposedly the prefiguration of Christ's Cross, signed on the forehead in baptism, in ashes on Ash Wednesday) as the sign placed on the doors of those houses wherein the first-born was to remain alive. The *tau* marked on the forehead of the elders by an angel is familiar in art, like the *tau* on the doorpost.

talks of the soul's honesty when it praises as a kind of necessary inner *rhyme* (sts. 2-3). It would be a great falsification to interpret any of Herbert's many discussions of craftsmanship in poetry in terms of the sincerity-is-enough sentimentality of a much later subjective criterion for good writing. The seventeenth was almost the last century to succeed in looking within without falling in head first and being submerged—probably because its thinkers had as a governing conception not reality conceived as within the individual consciousness, but, rather, the possibility of inner harmony with reality. When Herbert says 'Whereas if th'heart be moved,   Although the verse be somewhat scant,   God doth supplie the want', he does not say that the lack will not be apparent, but that God will mend it. We may wish he had called for this help in the rather low-creeping second stanza of this *Hymne*, but something at any rate has helped him to achieve a terse, witty, and compressed statement in the last two lines' hinted reproof and metrical jest: 'As when th'heart sayes (sighing to be approved)   *O, could I love!* and stops: God writeth, *Loved.*'

The same reservations must prevent us from over-interpreting 'The Posie' (p. 182), which begins 'Let wits contest' and ends ten lines later with

> Invention rest,
> Comparisons go play, wit use thy will:
> *Lesse then the least*
> *Of all Gods mercies*, is my posie still.

When we look into the source of this, Herbert's 'own Motto', we shall have confirmation of the fact that the title 'Jordan' is integrally a part of the poems which bear it, carrying both a deep personal and a full symbolic meaning. We shall also perceive yet once more that the persistent connecting of poetic theory with the search for humility is not fortuitous, but is related to the deepest springs of Herbert's thought. His friend Nicholas Ferrar of Little Gidding ends thus the preface to *The Temple* (p. 4):

We conclude all with his own Motto, with which he used to conclude all things that might seem to tend any way to his own honour;

Lesse then the least of Gods mercies.

Herbert's writing of poetry—even sacred poetry—was to a man of his acute self-knowledge one of these 'things'. We have looked at a bare few of the traces in his poems of his lifelong attempt to make *of literary creation—entire—*a devoted and self-forgetful religious act. The amazing difficulty of this is only perceptible to us when we stop to realize what is involved in making the total act of literary creation—including motive, process, character and subject-matter and style of resulting poems—*all* into the burning of the flames on the altar. One thinks twice before attributing lack of subtlety to Gerard Manley Hopkins, but his burning of his poems was a simpler answer. One would also think that Herbert's would be just one more way of burning up one's poems; indeed from the point of view of most aesthetic theory the excellence of his poetry is almost a troublesome fact. Few men have made literature of their humbly attained *successes* in the immolation of the individual will; we are accustomed to the beauty of certain renowned failures.

We see quite clearly, of course, throughout the whole body of his poetry his tireless search for a way of living, a mode of being, that will constitute an entire submission of his own will. That his willed creative acts, his poems, were to him one among other such attempts at submission is clear from his 'Dedication' (p. 4) of the edifice which was thus so truly *The Temple* and *The Church*:

> Lord, my first fruits present themselves to thee;
> Yet not mine neither: for from thee they came,
> And must return. Accept of them and me,
> And make us strive, who shall sing best thy name.

Not mine neither, and only thereby pure, is the burden of his chosen 'Motto', and *not mine neither*, the pure altar flame of love that returns whence it came, is an element in the meaning of the symbol Jordan when he uses it as the title of poems which deal with his gradual discovery of what this self-immolation meant.

Like any Renaissance personal 'device', Herbert's motto *Lesse then the least of Gods mercies* is obscure until we know its context or source. This source[41] is in Jacob's speech in Gen. xxxii. 10 (the chapter in which he wrestles with God and is given the name Israel), when in fear of his brother Esau Jacob prays for God's help and reminds Him of His promise:

I am not worthy *of the least of all the mercies* [marg. note: Hebrew: I am less than all, &c.] and of all the truth, which Thou hast shewed unto thy servant; *for with my staff I passed over this Jordan.*

To Herbert's sensitive conscience, his Jordans never stayed crossed, and though his poems are 'The Church' he tried in all humility to build, though they are the very purified speaking heart which was the altar to be built 'on that day

[41] As Hutchinson notes, an utterance of Paul's in Eph. iii. 8 is also pertinent: 'Unto me, who am *less than the least* of all saints, is this grace given, that I should preach among the Gentiles the unsearchable riches of Christ; and to make all men see what is the fellowship of the mystery, which from the beginning of the world *hath been hid in God*.' Herbert's poems touching the priesthood show that the long inner discipline of making himself sufficient to his office, and of making himself a good poet, are the same process. Both aspects of this process, in his active and his expressive life, are epitomized in the poem *Our life is hid with Christ in God* (p. 84), with its concentrated cosmological figure and hidden imagery of light and motion; the text, '*Coloss. 3. 3.*', is the one he had painted at his wife's seat in Bemerton Church.

when ye shall pass over Jordan', yet even so his poetry is
also the long record of his agony of spirit at seeing his
failures to think, be, and write as a 'very member of Christ',
an altar and tabernacle of Heavenly Love. There were rare
occasions when he dared to think he had 'passed over this
Jordan with his staff', had learned how at most to begin
to build that altar on the farther side of Jordan upon which
the workman's tool was not to be lifted. 'Jordan, I' and 'II'
are two such occasions. It is quite clear that Jordan, Christian symbol of redemptive purification and of entrance into
union with Christ as Heavenly Love incarnate, was Herbert's own symbol for this complex of ideas, and that he
thought of poetry as both the means and the fruit of such
a union.

The symbol was a 'public' one. We have observed in
Herbert's own poems its manifold and deep implications;
it should be made clear that such a complex of metaphorical meanings was also 'public', and no mere idiosyncrasy,
born of chance tie-ups between a number of Bible verses.
Because it was public it was understood, and not only
subtle but moving.

I have remarked upon the fundamental symbolic weight
of 'Jordan', in the Old Testament and the New, in connexion with the sacrament of Baptism and with the promise
of and the entrance into eternal life, in connexion with
Christ's Baptism and the soul or the Church as the bride,
especially when Baptism and Epiphany are paralleled. All
of these are connexions implying regeneration, cleansing,
dedication, redemptive salvation; they are too commonplace to need illustration. In iconography they are assumed
as immediately understandable. I take once more the short-
cut of looking only at texts so popular that they served as
iconographical handbooks.

The crossing of the Jordan into the Promised Land is

implicit in the grape-cluster picture with which the *Biblia Pauperum* accompanies Christ's Baptism. In the *Speculum humanae salvationis* Jordan is 'the figure of Holy Baptism' and passage over it by the children of Israel had this pre-figuration. Christ's Baptism is prefigured in the Ark of the Testament standing in Jordan while the people went over dry-shod (the twelve commemorating stones are the lives of the twelve apostles, even in Isidore). The other two types in this text are the sea of brass and Naaman's bathing in the Jordan, purifying him from the leprosy of the seven sins (see Plates X *a*, IX *b*; also XIII *a*).

Naaman as a type, popularized by appearance in Augus-tine, in Isidore, was given special attention because Christ Himself used as types of His saving mission the stories of Elias sent to the widow of Sarepta and Elisha cleansing Naaman in Jordan. Patristic commentary and homiletic literature naturally thence emphasizes these as prefigurations of Ecclesia, purified and united with Christ. This inter-pretation of Naaman's washing in Jordan took the firmer hold because the widow of Sarepta also appears constantly in iconography, her two sticks making a cross (paralleled with Christ carrying His Cross and Isaac his wood, in the *Biblia Pauperum*, the *Speculum*, the *Horae*; see Plate VIII *b*). But Ecclesia's uniting with Christ is always both corporate and individual, and Naaman is equally the single redeemed soul, washed of sins in *humilitas* and wedded to Love—'Naaman est peccator', as Hugo de S. Charo, for instance, says. So that it was himself Herbert saw in that spotted Naaman in the windows of King's (see Plate XVII), and those regenerating and dedicating waters were his own 'Jordan'.

The attachment of practically all the biblical references involved to the Lenten and Passion season is pertinent because Herbert's devotional use of that portion of early service books is more nearly certain. But in any case in the Anglican calendar of Herbert's day the readings of the Old Testament references to the unhewn altar raised after the passage over Jordan cluster around this season: Herbert read out Deut. xxvii on 6 March, Joshua viii on 13 March, Exod. xx on Easter Tuesday. Most striking of all, he had to read the impressive and terrible Commination Service— i.e. the public cursing of sinners in Deut. xxvii—on Ash Wednesday and once again before Easter.[42]

The very verses from Deut. xxvii which most strikingly command the erection of the altar across the Jordan were adapted to form a responsory: 'Vos qui transituri estis Jordanem, aedificate altare Domino, De lapidibus quos ferrum non tetigit . . .'; this was sung on the Monday in the fourth week of Lent, in the Roman and York Uses. It is worth mentioning that this responsory was used between portions of a sermon of Augustine's[43] which discourses on men's tendency to defile the temple of God by 'selling' therein; those who seek their own honour (cf. Ferrar on Herbert's Motto), these are they that sell; they magnify themselves not the Lord; Christ cast out from the temple even those who sold there what men could use for burnt offerings. Just such accusations does Herbert direct against himself, speaking of his poetic burnt offerings, written 'as if to sell', incompletely dedicated to Heavenly Love by a heart which only Christ could purify into a true temple. On the Monday

[42] Also twice again during the year. We know that at least one Elizabethan bishop (Grindal, in 1576) made an inquiry to ensure strictness in this point (see W. K. Clay, ed., *Liturgies and Occas. Forms of Prayer* . . . , Parker Soc., 1847, p. 239 n.). We also know from Walton that Herbert kept all services strictly, taking his family twice daily to church; he must read services privately if not publicly, even as deacon (i.e. before the time of his Bemerton priesthood).

[43] Tract. 10 on a Matins lesson for the day from John ii. The discussed portions of this and of the Ambrose sermon presently referred to may be found in any modern breviary; I used *Brev. Rom.*, Antwerp, ?1618. Cf. Augustine's rope of sins in the same tractate (*v.* Isa. v. 18) with Herbert's *rope* image in 'The Collar'.

preceding, Matins lessons include Luke iv and the sermon Ambrose based on it, dealing with Naaman and the widow of Sarepta as types of Ecclesia, the humble faithful ones singled out and saved by the baptismal cleansing. Herbert read Augustine's text, John ii, for Matins 15 March. I press no exact relationships. I think we should remember that men who had sermons to preach from the lessons assigned according to the Church year—Walton says Herbert always preached from the lesson for the day—not only knew patristic homiletic literature but probably did not scorn to use the glossed and amplified collections of biblical readings arranged according to the calendar. (Nor indeed the breviary, if they were men of Herbert's colour of belief, and with his pleasure in scriptural cross-reference and traditional symbolism.) The Anglican calendar was modelled on earlier Sarum usage, and frequently is identical with it, so that such relatively inexpensive glossed collections could be very convenient.

One could add to this quick review some of the appearances of allegorical comment on the Old Testament Jordan and altar passages that I have quoted, in authors commonly and easily known: in Isidore, connecting both the Joshua and Exodus passages with the 'living stones' of the 'spiritual house' in which 'spiritual sacrifices' are offered by the faithful (1 Pet. ii); in the *Glossa ordinaria*, quoting Gregory's *Moralia*; in Hugh of St. Victor (*Alleg. in vet. Test.*: Joshua 4 Kings). But the number of explanations of this and that aspect of the symbol would outstrip our patience to cite or read them, and it is surely already abundantly clear that Herbert has not made a fanciful personal use of a few scattered Bible passages, in poems into which I have thence read peculiar interpretations.

Yet, as in the case of every poet, the symbols Herbert inherited were as he used them transmuted into something

we call 'unique' and 'his own', for want of better terms.
When we have understood the common significance of his
symbol we have yet not read his poem, wherein it operates
to say something never said before, and never again since.
It is the paradox of all communication that a man can say
what is unique only because the language he says it in is
common to all, and it is the peculiarity of artistic communication that form is a pre-eminent component of meaning, so that this leap from the shared and known to the
unique and only partially knowable is assisted by instruments of a subtlety far beyond the crudities of any statable
shared sets of meanings. When Herbert uses the language
of symbols he uses a language rather formal than conceptual, and like rhythm, tones of the voice, proportion, it
is a language which can convey more than words can
enclose in their definable meanings. It can convey his own
painfully worked-out translation of known symbols into
living action, into thoughts and feelings at work within a
living human mind and felt within our own, not dead but
quick. We read of his understanding of human life and its
meaning, and the poem is that life itself, unique and im-
mediate, like our own.

The two Jordan poems, all the ten or a dozen poems
I have examined with them and several I have not, form
a distinguishable part of the living organism which is Herbert's functioning philosophy touching the uses of human
life. As in some delicate organic system in a breathing and
animate body, we see the same pulse beating in them, each
in a sense being 'part of' the other. The poems are not
'organized around the same idea'; in fact my necessarily
purely conceptual analysis has done them violence, and they
grew, rather than were organized, out of the same pattern
of symbols. Herbert is second to none in his achievement

of artistic unity within the bounds of the single short poem, and each of these is again part of the aesthetically notable larger unity of his whole book. But it is an organic unity which can take care of the phenomenon of growth and change, rather than a constructed unity wherein each single classifiable part has its inevitable place. It is conse-quently difficult, even perhaps falsifying, to divide off and treat single poems as discrete units—although an incom-plete understanding of a beautiful thing is worth having too.

Single ideas of Herbert's, even single metaphors, present us with the same difficulty; we may look at the leaf, the blossom, and the bole, but it is always the tree we gaze upon. This kind of organic unity will always characterize the work of a man who interprets life by the aid of meta-phor, because metaphor does not 'compare' one thing with another, it states that one thing is another. Metaphor (and allegory, which is metaphor) deals not with likenesses but with essences. So, of course, do symbols, the extreme of metaphors. They can reconcile seeming contradictions be-cause their terms can be 'different from' and 'the same as' simultaneously; nor is this in defiance of logic, for meta-phors deal with reality at the level of universals. When, as Sidney says, particulars 'are seen in their universal con-sideration' every part can be the whole without ceasing to be itself.

This is not an activity a man can ordinarily pursue starting from scratch and all on his own. Most great poets have used, rather than created, symbols, although they have seldom left them as they found them. The fact that *poetry has readers* is not the only factor in this. It is part of it, but no privately invented symbol has, to either poet or reader, the depth and the propulsive force of those which have had centuries of life in other men's minds. Herbert writes within a symbolic tradition, to him familiar, accepted and significant. It was not an esoteric tradition, but one in which his audience could follow him—some learnedly, some simply, some partially, some more fully, as with readers in all times, but all with a comprehension and hence a 'capacity to be struck' which outgoes ours. The fact that it is now an esoteric tradition damages the poems, for the things we lose are precious elements in the response to poetry—immediacy, richness, and subtlety of suggestion.

Part of this loss can be repaired. This is the cheerful side of the fact that it is a condition of literature and the other arts that meaning inheres in form. For we can learn about form, as men have always learned about it, through observation and repeated experience. If we are willing to learn Herbert's language we shall hear what he says, or most of it, being made able to experience the beauty and the power which are inextricably part of it. Since he says it in the language of metaphor it did not stop being true when certain meanings it may have had to him ceased to exercise power over men's minds. Metaphors cheat time in ways beyond a poet's foresight. The meanings we find still true, even in ways he did not foresee, are yet his meanings, but at a level so deep that no man knows or could say in cold conceptual formulation the reach and scope of them.

A Note on the accessibility of materials used, to the sixteenth- and seventeenth-century English reader

CERTAIN general caveats become apparent as one works with materials such as those used in this book over a long period of time, and with special attention to Renaissance education and scholarship, reading habits, and book ownership. We must not think the sixteenth- and seventeenth-century Protestant lay public as ignorant as is the modern Protestant lay public of patristic learning and medieval Christian literature; popular devotional and 'moral' literature was fed into from such sources constantly, and books printed earlier did not go out of existence automatically when sovereigns shifted ecclesiastical arrange- ments (e.g. the service books, school-books, glossed Bibles, meditations, and homilies). It is not possible to think that persons who showed no *seditious* tendencies were disturbed in their ownership and use of Catholic liturgy and literature of all types when one thinks of the case of Byrd, who as a pro- fessed Catholic with a recusant wife retained his eminent posi- tion in the Chapel Royal through all the storms and changes from the early Elizabethan years down to his death in 1623. Patristic learning, earlier liturgy, medieval treatises that re- ceived Continental or English printing, Catholic biblio- graphies, are not to be thought of as *recherché* to men with a sixteenth- or seventeenth-century clerical education, especially to men with Herbert's leanings (he is comparable, for example, to a Lancelot Andrewes). To say nothing of men like Donne from devout and outstandingly Catholic families, who re- mained Catholic on into the years of post-University study. Men whose working lives fell in *between* the periods of greatest tension were the more likely to use Catholic—and medieval— learning; in any case, they could not get along without it, and learning (as compared with dogmas held, popular observance or pulpit utterances) was slowly rather than suddenly protes- tantized. Medieval authors who seem to us beyond measure obscure were not only edited but anthologized and written up in the biographical dictionaries (e.g. everyone seems to know what Tritheim says). We no longer think of this period as without bibliographical tools (see Theo. Besterman, *Beginnings of Systematic Bibliography*, Oxford, 1936, and Archer Taylor, *Renaissance Guides to Books*, Berkeley, Calif., 1945), Cardinal Bellarmine's bibliography, 1613, being perhaps the most widely used, according to the latter. Our greatest omission in all this has been our tacit assumption of an eighteenth- or a twentieth-century lack of familiarity with patristic and medieval thought lying outside the stricter confines of scholastic philosophy—as being something very special, out-of-the-way, expert, and dust-covered.

It is equally dangerous to use our own knowledge and attitudes as a yard-stick in connexion with certain Christian Latin literary figures. Prudentius was set as a school author. A short session with the British Museum holdings, with special attention to the *Cathemerinon* or hymns which herein concern us, shows editions every few years from the earliest 1500's right through Herbert's life (gaps in the '80's and '90's); Erasmus's commentary, frequently adducing the 'allegorical' meanings for points in the hymns, reappeared in the handsome Weitzio edition of 1613 for instance. The existence of commentaries such as Erasmus's and others' may point out to us which parts of Prudentius were studied in schools (the *Cathem.* most). He appeared in anthologies, along with Venantius Fortunatus (including in both cases the pieces I make use of in this study). Two such books are the *Corpus omnium veterum poetarum latinorum*, 1611, and *Chorus Poetarum . . .*, 1616 (of these two the copies I used were owned by Ben Jonson). Both these authors appeared in yet more inclusive anthologies of medieval Christian Latin poetry, like the Protestant humanist Fabricius's *Poetarum veterum Ecclesiasticorum opera Christiana . . .,1564*. This has, besides these and many poets now little known, and besides the hymns of Ambrose and Sedulius, some thirty-five folio columns of 'Hymns of the church', according to season; Fabricius's notes regard not only authorship, metrics, or interpretation, but praise literary quality. Venantius Fortunatus is thus favoured of anthologists, besides separate editions of his Easter poem and Passion hymn (printed also, of course, in service books); he appeared alone in sixteenth- and seventeenth-century editions of his *Carmina*, &c., as well as in the more pretentious annotated Brouwer edition, containing also Rabanus Maurus, 1617, and the *Bibliotheca patrum* series, 1618.

This series was important, and its great folios cannot but remind us of Herbert's complaint about 'those infinite Volumes of Divinity, which yet every day swell, and grow bigger', writing in 1618 to his stepfather for money for books—'what Trades-man is there who will set up without his Tools?' I mention contemporary editions of single other authors in notes where I have used them. Augustine, Anselm, Bernard, and pieces ascribed to them, Honorius Augustodunensis, Hugh of Saint Victor, Hugo de S. Charo (St. Cher), and other glossators I have also treated where they came up, or see below on liturgical materials. Editions and translations of the first three were so numerous I must simply refer to the catalogue of any old or great collection like the Bodleian or British Museum. We are safe in assuming (without support) familiarity with Augustine, with 'Walafrid Strabo's' *Glossa ordinaria* and Nicholas of Lyra; I used the great standard glossed Bible still on the Duke Humphrey shelves at the Bodleian, containing *Glossa ord.*, Lyra, &c. (Lugduni, 1589). On these matters generally, see a book too recent for me to use (and dealing largely with more specialized commentaries): Arnold Williams, *The Common Expositor, an Account of the Commentaries on Genesis*, Chapel Hill, N.C., 1948. Herbert himself owned Augustine's works (see his will).

On reprinted liturgical manuals or collections thereof in the Renaissance, see a brief list in Cabrol, *Introd. aux études liturgiques*, Paris, 1907; books *on* the services, &c., of the Church are relevant here in connexion with ecclesiastical and biblical symbolism. G. Durandus's (William Durand's or Durant's)

Rationale divinorum officiorum was the most frequently reprinted of the several treatises of this type (see text above, Part II, n. 19; when editions exceed twenty we may certainly think of the book as easily accessible). For convenience, I use Migne's *Patrologia Latina* for the less frequently reprinted similar treatises, although I have consulted the older editions, such as that of Hugh of St. Victor's *Speculum ecclesiae* in M. Hittorp's *De divinis cathol. eccles. officiis*, Paris, 1610, and Joannes Belethus's (Belet's) *Rationale div. offic.*, Venice, 1561. Honorius's *Gemma animae*, for example, came out (1618; *Opera omnia*) in the series of the *Bibliotheca patrum*, even the lesser authors in which a clerical scholar like Herbert would have seen during a long university residence. We also know that Herbert had theological books bought abroad for him, and even his brother Lord Herbert owned books by Ferrari and Bauldry on Catholic liturgy (see *Oxf. Bibl. Soc.* v, pt. 2, 1937). Belethus's *Rationale*, reprinted ten or more times from 1553 to 1614, alone or with Durandus, is in *Patr. Lat.* 202. Honorius's *Gemma animae* is in *Patr. Lat.* 172, as is his *Sacramentarium*, a similar treatise somewhat differently organized; but his *Speculum eccles.* is of a different nature. Hugh of St. Victor's *Speculum ecclesiae* is in *Patr. Lat.* 177; because of frequent confusion in the attribution of this treatise I give the *incipit*, ch. 1, 'Ecclesia igitur in quam. . .'. The relatively uniform organization of such treatises makes reference by chapter headings sufficient.

It is my opinion that Herbert knew and used not only the *Horae* (as did Andrewes) and the missal, but even the breviary; he would have used all three for devotional purposes, using the breviary (as many clerics must have used it) also as a convenient, seasonally arranged, and less expensive repository of patristic selections, for sermon-making. However, nothing in these essays stands or falls by this opinion of mine. Editions of all service books were so extremely numerous (see STC: Liturgies) that they cannot have been hard to come at. Other Uses than Sarum must be looked for elsewhere than in the STC, but I have kept almost entirely to the Sarum Use as being still the easiest of access in England, and, of course, most closely related to the Anglican liturgy, which borrowed freely (or copied slavishly, if one prefers) from it. It should be borne in mind that the early seventeenth-century reader would have used a text (e.g. of the Latin hymns in the breviary) not showing the corrections, revisions of the Latinity, &c., made under Urban VIII and incorporated in the modern breviary.

Sequences and hymns of the church, even those not to be read in editions of famous authors (like Ambrose, Gregory, Rabanus, Prudentius, Ven. Fortunatus) were not accessible only in service books. The most important single category is the group of school-books used in the teaching of Latin—the *Expositio hymnorum* and *Expositio sequentiorum*. Though early, these were numerous; there is nothing unlikely in the idea that a boy like Donne received part of his training in Latin grammar and 'modern' vocabulary through such books (see STC: Liturgies, and E. Pafort in *Library*, xxvi (1946), pp. 227 ff.). In addition, certain names are to be noticed in connexion with the publishing and 'exposition' of this important *genre* of Christian lyric poetry. Jodocus Badius Ascensius, the printer, remembered for Erasmus's praising him above Budaeus, published and commented, *literaliter et figuraliter*, on the sequences of the Sarum Use and hence presumably for the English public. This last limitation does not apply to the commentary of Torrentinus, author also of a *Dictionarium poeticum* or handbook which saw edition after edition (even one in the 1780's!); or to the commentary of Joannes Adelphus, known through his activities as translator (of Erasmus *et al.*) and editor, or in connexion with the famous Calepine *Dictionarium*. These last two publishings of sequences not only provide small inexpensive texts of pieces typically filled with traditional Christian symbolism, but comment at length thereupon. (For examples connected with matters treated above: Under the famous *Laudes crucis*: the two trees paralleled, Christ *ascendens sanctam crucem*, to undo Adam's act, Christ as the fruit, the Seth story. Under *Psallat ecclesia*: the ark of the Church and of the Virgin's womb, Melchisedec 'rex Salem'. Under *Iocundare plebs fidelis* and *Coeli enarrant*, the apostles 'irrigating' the people, &c., &c.).

One extremely important name in connexion with Renaissance publication and appreciation of medieval liturgical poems is that of J. Clichtoveus, whose very full *Elucidatorium Ecclesiasticum* was printed a good many times between 1515 and 1556 (Cologne, 1732, for that matter), and who especially appreciated the sequences of Adam of St. Victor. Vérard published the *Hymnes en français*, but translation was not the normal way in which these poems became better known; motets would be more important. But antiphon texts were far more commonly set to music than hymns, and music is most important for fixing certain biblical details and liturgical symbols, movingly, in particular often highly allegorical contexts. As a carrier of tradition music is always to be reckoned with; the greater musical literacy of sixteenth and seventeenth century readers and writers is a byword. One further difference in connexion with sacred poetry should be mentioned: to men like Herbert and Donne, not only were many of these pieces famous ones, or known as only schoolbooks are known, but also the liturgical arrangement according to seasons, feasts, and services was second nature, offering a clear path through what may seem to us an uncharted wilderness of sacred Latin poetry. This seemingly simple point is of considerable importance, not only in thinking of sources and familiarity, but in studying the corpus of divine poems left by these authors themselves.

The extreme frequency of editions in all languages (and mixtures thereof) of the *Horae* (Primers), and their lay ownership, are wellknown facts. I could perhaps save the time of others who would be interested to look at typological series in illustrated printed *Horae* without travelling the whole maze of these books in any great library, by appending STC and other numbers for a judicious small selection of *Horae* containing typological illustrations (see also above, Part II, note 24). STC covers only Sarum Use; since frequency of editions makes month and day necessary for accurate identification, I give examples of other Uses with either very summary identification, by printer, or number in Proctor for convenience in British Museum or Bodley: STC 15879, 15885,15909, 15910; Proctor 8045, 8046, 8182, †8465; Vérard 1508, Kerver 1497, 1503, 1506, 1513, 1526. Various Venetian examples can be quickly located in d'Essling (e.g. 1517, 1524, 1544, &c.). Cf. also STC 6429 ff., the Book of Christian Prayers ('Queen Eliza-beth's Prayerbook'). Typological cuts also got into books like *L'art de bien vivre* (Vérard, Dec. 1492; May 1503 [STC 791]), and Vérard copies the *Biblia Pauperum* set-up in *Les Figures du Vieil Testament & du Nouuel* (B. Mus. C. 22. b. 7). If applications of Psalms or O.T. readings, or juxtapositions of materials, prayers, hymns, &c., occur in *Horae* and Primer, they must be thought of as very common, the pictures turned over as a child in the library at home.

The *Biblia Pauperum* is so well known as the most famous of early block books that I shall only cite as a way to discover manuscripts and editions J. Henrik Cornell, *Biblia Pauperum*, Stockholm, 1925. The *Speculum humanae salvationis* can be studied in J. Lutz and P. Perdrizet's edition, 2 vols., Mulhouse, 1907, with Latin text, French fifteenth-century translation, and complete reproduction of one manuscript. Besides the manu-scripts and the block-book edition, there were German (and Swiss) editions and translations, five or more appearances of the Julien French translation, *Le Mirouer de la redempcion humaine*, from the amplified German version, *Spiegel menschlicher Behalt-niss*, containing patristic excerpts, sermons, epistles and gospels for the relevant day of the church year, &c. There was a Vérard edition; there was an English translation (in a Huth MS. printed for the Roxburghe Club).

A Note on conventions of quoting used in this book

HERBERT'S poems are cited throughout from the edition of
F. E. Hutchinson, *The Works of George Herbert* (Oxford, 1941:
Clarendon Press); since their order is all but impossible to
remember I consistently insert page references in parentheses
(to pages on which the poems begin, except with long poems
where confusion would result. For 'The Sacrifice' line numbers
are given.) I have not thought it worth the annoyance it would
cause readers to indicate repeatedly that it is 'my italics' which
point up words or phrases in quoted images.

Patristic references which can be easily identified and found
in Migne's *Patrologia Latina* or other standard editions, or in
translations, are not elaborated; for occasional specific passages,
columns in Migne are given to save a student trouble, the
abbreviation *Patr. Lat.* then being used. Ordinarily the usual
titles and divisions (chapters, &c.) suffice for identification.
With Bible commentaries, Isidore, the *Glossa ordinaria* (in *Patr.
Lat.* 113–14, *s.v.* Walafrid Strabo) and similar texts, the biblical
reference is sufficient, bearing in mind the archaic 1, 2 and
3, 4 Kings for 1, 2 Samuel and 1, 2 Kings, and the difference in
Vulgate numbering of the Psalms (I use the Book of Common Prayer numbering, and text).

I modernize the thorn, eth, and yak in Middle English quotations. References to Carleton Brown's editions of *English Lyrics
of the xiiith Century*, *Religious Lyrics of the xivth Century*, *Religious Lyrics of the xvth Century* (Oxford, 1932, 1924, 1939,
Clarendon Press) are made by number of poem and by in-
dicating the century (e.g. xiii: 100, xiv: 100).

References to the Sarum Missal are to the translation by
Frederick E. Warren, 2 vols., London, 1911 (de la More Press);
references to the Sarum Breviary are to *Breviarium ad usum* . . .

Sarum, ed. F. Proctor and C. Wordsworth, 3 vols., Cambridge, 1882, 1879, 1886. The precautions taken to show a student the exact provenance of liturgical quotations or usages are these: whether mentioned details were part of the Anglican or the Catholic liturgy will be clear from their names or my references. When I refer to 'Epistle', 'Gospel' or 'Lesson', these belong to the Anglican Holy Communion, Matins, or Evensong; however, choices had been consistently taken over from Sarum Use by the Book of Common Prayer (BCP). References to the 'Sarum Brev.' or 'Sarum M.' *alone*, however, are to be found in those earlier English Catholic service books. It was necessary to check usages against the calendar as Herbert used it. A fair number of changes in 1662 make the modern BCP an insuffi-cient guide (more especially as to daily Matins lessons, and con-trary to statements in histories of the BCP); however, Herbert's calendar was almost completely that of 1561, conveniently found in Parker Soc., 1847, *Liturgies . . . in the reign of Queen Elizabeth*, ed. W. K. Clay.

Since I have referred to various Early English Text Society editions simply by number of volume in order to save awkward-ness and over-many footnotes, especially in Part I above, I append here a brief list of EETS texts to which I have referred either summarily or else fairly often. References are to Original Series unless Extra Series is specified.

EETS 15. *Political, Religious and Love Poems*, ed. F. J. Furnivall, 1866.

EETS 24. *Hymns to the Virgin and Christ. . .* , ed. F. J. Furnivall, 1867.

EETS 46. *Legends of the Holy Rood*, ed. Richard Morris, 1871.

EETS 57, 59, 62, 66, 68, 99, 101. *The Cursor Mundi*, ed. Richard Morris, 1874–93.

EETS 98, 117. *Minor Poems of the Vernon MS.*, ed. Carl Horstmann, F. J. Furnivall, 1892, 1901.

EETS 103. *History of the Holy Rood-tree*, ed. A. S. Napier, 1894.

EETS 105, 109. *The Prymer; or, Lay Folks Prayer Book*, ed. H. Littlehales, 1895-7.

EETS 124. *Twenty-six Political and Other Poems*, ed. J. Kail, 1904.

EETS 200. *Speculum Sacerdotale*, ed. E. H. Weatherly, 1936.

EETS *extra ser.* 27. *The English Works of John Fisher*, ed. H. E. B. Mayor, 1876.

EETS *extra ser.* 71. *The Towneley Plays*, ed. by G. England and A. W. Pollard, 1897.

EETS *extra ser.* 80. *Lydgate's Minor Poems: The Two Nightingale Poems*, ed. O. Glauning, 1900.

EETS *extra ser.* 96. *Mirk's Festial*, Part I, ed. Theodor Erbe, 1905.

A Note for students interested in certain types of texts

THIS Note gives certain modern time-saving helps, especially in cases where modern editions, collections, &c., were not cited, as irrelevant to the question of accessibility to earlier readers (but see also that Note).

A number of the commonest medieval hymns and sequences are conveniently accessible with translations in *Hortus Con-clusus: A Series of Mediaeval Latin Hymns*, complete in ten parts, ed. Stephen A. Hurlbut (Washington, 1936: Mount St. Albans Press). The cited translation of the Sarum Missal, covering, of course, only Sundays and feast days, provides chiefly the sequences, but Sarum hymns may be read in *The Psalter or Seven Ordinary Hours of Prayer* . . . , London, 1852, or in *The Breviary of the Renowned Church of Salisbury*, rendered into English according to the use of the Society of the Holy Trinity, Devonport (London, 1889; cf. the Portiforium of 1556, STC 15842). The *Roman Breviary* was translated into English by John 3rd Marquess of Bute, 4 vols., London, 1908 (Blackwood). Since the last two use translations by Newman, *et al.*, the modernization under Urban VIII must be taken into consideration. A translation of the *Horae B.V.M.* is con-veniently to hand in the works of Corneille, although, of course, the inclusions in early *Horae* show wide variation. A Latin breviary of the Use of York is reprinted by the Surtees Society.

The large terrain of liturgical poetry (and even some relevant patristic commentary) is usefully opened up for a reader without large stores of reference works by Archbishop Trench's *Sacred Latin Poetry* (London, 1886: Kegan Paul and Trench). But care must be taken about following any modern treatment or collection (such as Mone, Daniel, or Drêves), for the question of availability to Renaissance readers must always be checked. Very false notions of what was 'traditional' can arise from looking at materials which were known to the medieval cen-turies and lit up by the scholarship of the nineteenth, but quite dark to men that lived between. For Adam of St. Victor: E. Misset and P. Aubry, *Les Proses d'Adam de St. V.* (Paris, 1900), are careful about attributions, and selective, whereas D. S. Wrangham's three volumes of translations (London, 1881) include the much larger number of sequences still thought to be Adam's in the Renaissance. Translations and texts, in Clichtoveus's order, appear in an Appendix in Vol. III of Barthélemy's translation of Durandus. For this and another (partial) modern translation of Durandus's treatise see above, Part II, note 19.

On the vast numbers of *Horae* editions see STC or John Hoskins, *Sarum and York Primers...*, London, 1901. However, other uses than Sarum must be considered when iconographical series are in question, for such books were no doubt partly owned for their pictorial interest. Neither the bibliographies including many uses (like Bohatta or Lacombe), nor Hoskins, give sufficient assistance on character of illustration—on the presence or absence of the series of typological cuts, for instance. Nor can this be surely ascertained from A. W. Pollard's article, 'The Illustrations in French Books of Hours, 1486–1500'—useful nevertheless, though the British Museum press marks he gives have since been changed (in *Bibliographica*, 1897). Material still not brought together elsewhere is to be found in M. R. James's introduction to *A Book of Old Testament Pictures . . . now in the Morgan Library*, printed for the Roxburghe Club in 1927, and Emile Mâle's three volumes are still essential for iconographical study in this especial area (*L'Art religieux du xii* siècle, . . . *du xiii* siècle, . . . *de la fin du moyen âge, en France*. Of these there are various editions and partial translations, and in the text above I have rather assumed familiarity with them and avoided repetition than made any attempt to notice the many analogues and supporting evidences).

A Note for Students

There is by design no Index in this book. It is not amenable to use as a dictionary of symbols or as a repertory of specific sources. I have therefore cited cross references to a possibly annoying degree.